Big Bad Boss

Moon Mad

Werewolves of Wall Street
Book 2

Renee Rose

Lee Savino

Midnight Romance Publishing

Want FREE books?

Receive a slew of free Renee Rose books: Go to **http://subscribepage.com/alphastemp** to sign up for Renee Rose's newsletter and receive a free books. In addition to the free stories, you will also get special pricing, exclusive previews and news of new releases.

Download a free Lee Savino book from www. leesavino.com

Chapter One

Madi

I trek through the woods, fresh snow crunching under my feet. The sun shines, refracting on the snow to make a billion tiny diamonds. I'm having a Dr. Zhivago moment, stunned by the beauty of the ice and nature-made snow sculptures all around me. I stop to investigate an icicle hanging from a tree, but a low growl makes me freeze.

I whirl to find I'm surrounded by a half-dozen giant wolves–snarling, angry, probably hungry wolves.

They advance on me slowly, their big paws sinking into the snow with each step. The largest one–the tan one with a black streak running from chin to chest leaps at me, and I scream–

I kick off the bedcovers.

A strong arm bands around me. "Hey," a deep familiar voice reaches me, and the forest fades to a bedroom.

I jerk awake with a gasp.

"You okay?" Brick spoons me, his large body molded around mine.

"Oh my God." I sit up, shoving my hair from my face. We're in the guest room in the Berkshires. I can't tell what time it is. "I dreamt wolves were chasing me in a snowstorm."

Brick sits up, too, and I tug the sheet up to my armpits, suddenly aware I'm naked in a bed with my billionaire boss.

"Come here." He hauls me into his lap, cradled sideways, my shoulders leaning back against one of his arms, my knees across his lap.

I'm shocked he wants to cuddle. Is this still a dream? I can't seem to orient myself.

He tugs down the sheet and cups one of my breasts, like my body belongs to him. "I'm sorry about the wolves. And the blizzard. And for driving you out into it."

I lift my brows. "Wow. Another apology? That's two trophies I'm having made."

He brushes a thumb across one of my nipples, and I relax into him at the sensual touch.

"Has anyone ever been attacked by wolves on your property before?"

"No. They don't attack humans."

"Oh, they were going to attack me." The memory of the wolves surrounding me comes back, only now it's muddled by the dream. Which one was real? I'm not usually so confused.

"Tell me what happened." Brick is still toying with my nipple. There's a familiarity between us like we're long-time lovers.

"I was out in the blizzard. I thought I heard you calling me, so I tried to yell back, but my voice was giving out. I found a branch to bang against a tree to make noise."

"That was good thinking."

"Then suddenly, there were six wolves surrounding me, howling. One of them even came at me."

Brick seems to stiffen. Finally he's actually giving my experience some credence. "*Came at you, how?*"

"It came right up to me and almost sat on my foot."

He relaxes. "That doesn't sound aggressive, Windows. Was it showing you fangs? Growling?"

"Well, no."

"What did it look like?"

"It was huge. Tan with black markings. It had a streak of black that ran from chin to chest." I draw a line down my throat to show him.

Brick relaxes some more. "A female?"

"I don't know. Are you familiar with these wolves?"

"Oh, I know them. That pack has been in these woods longer than any human."

"And no one's ever been eaten?"

"Never." He sounds amused. Like me being afraid of wolves is a cute quirk of mine and not a legit danger. "It sounds to me like the wolf was trying to comfort you. Have you ever had a dog come and sit against your leg? It's a sign of solidarity."

I wrinkle my brow and give him a quick glance. "I don't think so." Now I'm not so sure. Was the wolf really going to attack me? Maybe I was confused.

Brick pinches my nipple and flips me onto my back. I'm instantly wet. Totally ready. "You don't have to be afraid of the big, bad wolf." He straddles my waist and pins my wrists to the bed as he nips the soft side of my breast.

I gasp and arch into him. "Just the Big, Bad Boss?"

"Definitely him." He swirls his tongue around my nipple.

3

I grip his head, running my fingers through his hair. "Am I still in trouble?"

"So much." His voice is gravelly with lust. "I'm going to fuck you into submission, Windows."

I arch. "Won't happen," I choke, but my hips roll beneath him, seeking firm contact.

"The submission or the fucking?"

I spread my legs, and our hips line up. "Submission."

* * *

I wake up on the edge of an orgasm. This time there's no confusion. I'm not in bed with Brick Blackthroat in the Berkshires because I left there Thanksgiving night.

I'm horny, alone, and in my childhood bedroom at my mom's place.

Apparently the dream within a dream was my subconscious working overtime to process what happened over Thanksgiving.

I'm sure part of the problem was the way I left.

After Thanksgiving dinner, I was expecting–or maybe just hoping for–another round with the Big Bad Boss. Instead, he disappeared outside with his buddies, and then Billy showed up to tell me that the weather had cleared, and John had readied the helicopter.

That was it. No closure. No goodbye. I just get hustled out to the helipad by the guy who seems to despise me, and then I'm back in the city in time for pumpkin pie with my mom and brother.

Apparently, as soon as the storm cleared, it was time for "the help" to leave.

I haven't heard a word from Brick–or maybe I should go back to thinking of him as Blackthroat–since.

I really need to talk to Aubrey. We've texted, but I need a full convo with the bestie. I pick up my phone and call.

"Oh my God, girl, tell me everything!" That's how she answers. Because my short texts–*I didn't quit* and *Slept with the boss*–were not nearly enough information. She and her mom are in New Jersey with her aunt and uncle for the holiday.

"Ugh. I don't know where to start."

Aubrey instantly sobers. "Wait, I thought things were good. What happened?"

Tears sting the back of my eyes. "They were good." The memory of Brick spooning me to warm my body, apologizing, and the mad, crazy sex flood my brain with remembered pleasure. But then there was getting sent home without so much as a goodbye. "So I texted you about me getting lost in the storm and the sexy times."

"Right."

"And then I stayed for Thanksgiving dinner, which was weird and awkward, but not because of me–at least I don't think. Because Brick and his mom don't get along, and his sister invited her. Supposedly he was a dick to me partly because he didn't want me to see his fucked up family."

"Oh, wow."

"Yeah. But then right after Thanksgiving dinner, he and all his dude-bros go outside and talk, and then he disappears. The next thing I know, Billy White comes in and says the weather cleared enough to get me home for Thanksgiving, but I had to leave right then."

"Okay."

"I asked where Brick was, but he said he'd gone for a run, which was obviously a lie because who goes for a run in the dark with a full stomach when it's freezing out?"

"Oh, shit."

5

"I know."

"So what did you do?"

"So I left! I mean, I obviously didn't belong there. Clearly they didn't want me there, or they wouldn't be rushing me off."

"Or maybe they just thought you wanted to spend Thanksgiving with your own family and were trying to get you there considering you'd already sacrificed most of your holiday for work."

Huh. Aubrey, the voice of reason.

"Yeah, maybe." I know I can be touchy about the class-difference thing. Did I make it all up?

No, I don't think so. But now I'm not sure.

"So how was the sex?" Aubrey puts a suggestive purr in her voice, steering me back to the good part.

"Ah-mazing. Insane. Incredible."

"So you got something out of it. That's good."

"I did...but I don't think I should do it again."

"Why not?"

"It feels too dangerous. I don't want to catch feelings because I already know how these things end."

"Wait, whoa. What does that mean?"

"I mean there's no way I'm ever going to actually end up with a guy like Brick Blackthroat. People may dally outside their social strata, but that's all it is. A dalliance."

"So you're saying because you're not going to marry this guy, you can't enjoy some hot sex and helicopter rides?"

Something twists beneath my ribs. I don't want to give up any of it.

But I have to. It would only end in disaster. And I'm not the type to take risks when I know they won't pay off.

"No more sex with the boss," I say firmly.

6

"Okay," Aubrey agrees. "I say you keep torturing him. Wear the dresses *and* withhold sex. He'll go nuts."

Somehow, that doesn't feel right either.

I don't want to withhold anything from Brick Blackthroat.

But that is my most dangerous thought of all.

I end the call with Aubrey and throw on a robe to pad out to the kitchen where my mom and Brayden are demolishing the Sunday crossword. I stand over their shoulders, offering answers to the remaining clues.

"Bruh, it's no fun when you're around," Brayden grumbles. "Between you and Mom, it goes too fast."

My mom, who has a PhD in literature, kicks butt at the *New York Times* crosswords, but Brayden and I can hold our own. I guess all of us enjoy a challenge.

"What was the Blackthroat estate like?" Brayden asks between bites of leftover pecan pie.

"I didn't see the property because of the blizzard, but the cottage was built in the Gilded Age. It's a forty-four room mansion with giant stone fireplaces and ornate carved wood trim." I got some of those details from Brick's mom, Catherine, when we chatted in the living room.

My mom's lips turn down with judgment. Sometimes I forget where I get my love-hate relationship with money. My mom is one of those people, like Aubrey, who believe all rich people are greedy, environment-destroying, anti-socialist assholes who make their money by stomping on the backs of the underprivileged. I know her relationship with my biological father contributed greatly to that view.

I've embraced that philosophy for the most part, except I also secretly enjoy money. I like my new six-figure salary–although I'm regretting asking him to double it. His entire executive team now knows that I've slept with him, so getting a hundred thousand dollar raise probably won't sit well with any of them.

My pride would be wounded having people think I slept my way to a raise rather than worked my ass off for it.

I did like wearing a twenty thousand dollar gown to a charity ball, even though it wasn't *me*. It was fun to play the part for the night. To ride in the limo and the helicopter. All of it has been fun to experience, even if it's just to laugh and make fun of the rich behind their backs. I'm not bedazzled by Blackthroat's wealth, but I definitely enjoy the perks.

I guess there's something inauthentic about my own relationship with money. A conflict I haven't figured out how to resolve. I try to remind myself that money isn't real. It is power Blackthroat and the old bluebloods wield, and power can be abused or used for good. Rejecting it altogether doesn't fix or resolve social injustice or disparities between the classes.

"I can't believe you just ordered up his helicopter. Are you allowed to use it for other things?"

"No. God no. I only did it because it was an emergency. Blackthroat was definitely pissed. Although I guess he was more mad about how dangerous it was with the blizzard than the liberties I took ordering it."

My mom goes still and stares at me with a look of alarm.

Crap on a cracker. Now she probably suspects there's something more to our relationship than assistant-boss.

"Only because it meant I got stranded there and had to join his family for Thanksgiving," I add quickly. As I say the words that I know will reassure and redirect my mom, I realize how much her thinking influenced me in that moment when Blackthroat blew up at me. That was the conclusion I jumped to, rather than the one in which my boss secretly cared about my safety and was cranky that I put myself in danger.

But maybe the latter is just a Cinderella fantasy. It's honestly hard for me to discern which statement is more true. I'm too involved in this situation to trust my own sense of deduction and logic.

"Yeah, how was that?" Brayden asks.

"Awkward. Super awkward. I'm glad to be home." Sort of.

Obviously, Brick wanted me gone. This was nothing but a fling. Sure, we got close for one second, but in the end, we're from different worlds. He's a billionaire. I'm the help. We're boss-employee. His family home over the holidays was no place for me to be.

So, I left the Berkshires–and not because Billy White ran me out. I left because I knew it was the safest choice for my heart. Developing any expectations of Blackthroat that can be easily dashed is a recipe for disaster. And I'm far too careful a planner for foibles like that.

Tomorrow, I plan to go in and pretend nothing ever happened. Back to being the perfect assistant to the big bad boss.

Brick

My private sports club is a lot like any other upscale gym, with one main difference. Everyone here is a shifter.

There's a werelion in the corner, swinging a kettlebell. Another two shifters–one smelling like a cat and the other like a bull or maybe buffalo–spotting each other at the bench press.

And a werebear in the boxing ring across from me.

The air is thick and humid with the scent of shifters and good, clean sweat. The place echoes with snarls and the occasional roar.

Like the rest of the gym, the fighting ring has a rule: no animal forms allowed. If you want to let your animal out, you do so on private land. Anyone losing control like that gets kicked out. But I can feel my wolf testing my control, trying to break free.

A bell rings, and I launch myself towards my opponent. He comes out swinging. We meet in the middle of the ring, jabbing and punching while keeping light on our feet.

He sneaks a strike past my defenses, and my body rocks with the blow. Pain washes through me, and I relish it. Anything to distract from the empty feeling that's gnawed on my insides since Thanksgiving.

My opponent is Darius Medevev, CEO of an up-and-coming hedge fund and good friend. My top wolves–Billy, Nickel, Jake, Vance and Sully–are all members here, but I came in this morning because I knew they were already at the office. I haven't wanted to see them since they faced me down in the snow and told me to send Madi away.

I hike back my fist and let it fly. Darius takes the punch, grunts, and gives it back as good as he gets. He's over six feet tall and built. The perfect opponent, except my wolf wishes it were Billy in the ring.

Get rid of Madison, he said, *before she brings this entire pack down.*

I throw another punch and miss. I try again with a right hook, and it glances off Darius' side.

My sisters.

Jab. Jab. Cross.

The pups.

I feint right, but Darius doesn't fall for it.

Get rid of her.

With a roar, I rush forward and smash Darius' face. There's a crunch, and he staggers back, blood pouring from his nose. My wolf snarls, wanting to chase him down for the kill. I force myself back to my corner.

Darius sets his long fingers on either side of his nose and snaps the cartilage back into place. The blood has already stopped flowing. Shifters heal quickly, and if we don't set our broken bones immediately, they'll heal wrong. Nothing worse than breaking your leg, limping back home only for your dad to chew you out while the pack healer breaks it again.

My father knew I had to be tough and strong. He knew that I'd be in an arena just like this fighting for my life every-day. I just didn't realize I would have to fight my best friends.

You need to get rid of her.

Billy only said what needed to be said. I did my duty and had him send Madi away. But that doesn't mean I don't still want to go after her and destroy anyone who stands in my way.

"Dude," Darius calls. "I don't know if you realize this, but your eyes have been glowing for the past five minutes. Your wolf is showing."

Fuck. I turn away and run my tongue over my teeth. My canines are dangerously sharp. I brace myself against the ropes and force my wolf back down. He snarls and retreats, but I don't feel any calmer. There's an empty ache deep in my gut.

"You want to go another round?" Darius asks.

I shake my head and glance at the giant clock fixed to the wall, a reminder that I have tens of thou-sands of people counting on me every second of every day. I can forget myself for a few minutes, but that's all.

Duty. Honor. Pack. I was raised to uphold my pack's legacy. And now I want to throw it all away. Chase after my human assistant like a smitten puppy.

And I hate myself for it. I can't be weak like this. The fate of my entire pack rests on my shoulders. They need a strong alpha to lead them. One wrong move, and the Adalwulfs will be at our throats.

Mating a human would be seen as weak. Doing so would let down my pack and my entire bloodline. My children wouldn't inherit the throne. But at worst, Aiden would exploit the weakness, poach my pack members, and leave the Blackthroat line, including Auggie and April, exposed for a kill.

So while I'm alpha, I could never claim a human mate. And right now, things are too precarious to consider a regime change. If I stepped down, the Adalwulfs would take it as a sign of weakness, and come after us with everything they have. We barely survived my father's death. We lost the company and only held onto the pack because my inner circle rallied around my leadership. Together we were an impenetrable force.

Things are still not stable. Right now, I'm the only one who can lead us. It's the role I was born for. I can't just walk away.

No matter how much I'm tempted.

Whenever I waver, I imagine my nephew Auggie. Laughing, running from his mother, tumbling down a snowy hill. If the Adalwulfs attacked, they wouldn't be merciful. They'd slit his throat and leave him dead in the snow.

They've done it before. They've wiped whole packs off

the map. My father told those horror stories around the campfire so we'd remember why the Adalwulfs are our enemies.

They're completely ruthless, and if they see me as weak, they'll come after us. Aiden Adalwulf could challenge me for the alpha position in another form of hostile takeover. This one with more disastrous consequences than losing billions of dollars and control of the company.

My wolf hates that I sent Madi away, but he understands. He's as torn as I am.

At least I will still see her at work. Unless she actually did quit. After the way Billy hustled her out of the manse, I wouldn't blame her.

"I need to get into the office." My voice comes out a growl. The sign that my wolf is close. I dip out of the ring and trot to a nearby table stacked with clean white towels. I grab one and rub my face with it.

Darius follows.

"Good fight," I say, and my voice sounds better.

"Thanks. You were distracted."

I grunt.

"Is it Benson?"

"No. Benson is almost wrapped."

"Good." Darius tosses me a water bottle and grabs one for himself. "I heard the Adalwulfs took a chunk out of it."

"Yeah, they grabbed a bunch of shares. When we take control, Aiden will have a vote, until we force him out."

"Aiden Adalwulf," Darius says slowly. "Isn't he your cousin?"

"Yes." Cousins, we were both ruthlessly groomed to lead a pack. The irony is Aiden Adalwulf is the one person on Earth in a position to understand the incredible pressure I'm under. Not that I'd ever admit a hint of weakness to him. One misstep, and he'd coolly slit my throat.

"You know what they're saying about you, right?"

"Who?"

"The Adalwulfs. Their seeress has a new prophecy about you."

I go cold. The Adalwulf pack has always had a seeress who advises the Alpha. Her prophecies have always given their pack an edge. "What?"

"Oh, you hadn't heard? It's something like, *The Black-throat king has a weakness.* I assume that refers to you."

The words hit me harder than any of his previous punches, but I'm careful to keep my expression blank.

The prophecy is obviously about me and Madison. Fuck.

"I need to get to the office."

"You need to go for a run. Let your wolf out." There's sober concern on Darius' face.

If I were smart, I'd take his friendly advice and head right back to the Berkshires.

But I have to see her.

* * *

Madi

Monday morning, Brick steps off the elevator looking... different. His hair is still wet, like he just showered, and he has an aggressive edge to him. Like the four-day weekend had the opposite effect of a normal man's vacation. He definitely didn't return relaxed.

I predict at least three people will get fired today.

Hopefully, I won't be one of them.

His nostrils flare as he stalks in and heads straight for me.

If I were an employee less confident in my work, I'd already be packing my things in a box based on his murderous look.

But instead of tearing into me, he slams a Starbucks cup down on my desk. Well, as much as one can slam a paper cup.

The phone is ringing, so I quickly answer it while holding Blackthroat's gaze. "Mr. Blackthroat's office, please hold." I press the hold button and drop the receiver into the cradle.

"Good morning, sir." I go with smooth and professional.

Not, I-just-fucked-the-boss-this-weekend.

He glowers at me but seems short on words. Instead, he picks up the coffee cup and moves it closer to me.

I stare up at him with shock. Did he actually *buy me a coffee*? I rotate the cup to read the label. It's a vanilla latte. The Big Bad Boss brought me coffee. Color me...*shocked*?

"I have to smell it every day," he says dryly, like my coffee choice offends him.

I had a game plan today–to play it professional. I was prepared for him to either do the same or to act overly-familiar, at which point I would initiate a conversation about us returning to boss-employee relations.

What I didn't plan on was this...*weird*...behavior.

"You're staying." He practically snarls it. Like we were having an argument, and this is his rebuttal.

I pick up the coffee. "You bought me a coffee to make sure I don't quit?" As far as gestures go, it's pretty meager, and I let that opinion leak into my tone.

"No." He looks grim. This is definitely his you're-getting-fired face.

Nothing makes sense this morning.

He looks down at the coffee like he has absolutely no idea how it got there. "The coffee is..." –he gives an impatient jerk of his head– "I don't know what the coffee is for, but you're staying. I need you–as my assistant. Understood?"

Why do I feel like I'm getting spanked by the boss instead of praised? I pride myself on reading my employer, but this morning, I'm at a complete loss.

"I'm here, aren't I?" I pick up the coffee and take a sip, holding his dark gaze. "Sir."

Blackthroat makes a low growling sound in his throat, turns on his heel, and heads into his office without further comment.

"Thanks for the coffee, Big Bad," I snark under my breath.

I swear I hear him say "You're welcome" from the other side of the door, but that would be impossible because there's no way he could hear me from in there.

I pick up the phone. "Thank you for holding, how may I help you?"

"Oh Madi, good. I'm glad you're there. It's Ruby Blackthroat."

"Oh, hi! Sorry to keep you holding. Br–er, Mr. Blackthroat–just walked in."

"I'm actually calling for you." Ruby's voice is warm, like we're friends now. Like I'm not just the help anymore. "I wanted to make sure you were okay after nearly going into hypothermia on Thanksgiving."

Well, that's nice. At least someone in the Blackthroat family acts like a normal human being.

"I am. I'm fine, thank you. And it was great to get home in time to have pie with my family that night. Sorry I didn't say a proper goodbye. I was sort of hustled out when there was a break in the weather."

"Oh, I know. No need to apologize."

"Thank you for everything–lending me your clothes, and–"

"Of course, of course," she cuts in. "I just wanted to say...well, I'm glad Brick has you–I mean someone like you. He runs through assistants faster than I use up Post-it Notes, and I'm the queen of Post-its, so it's nice that he can rely on you."

Okay, now she's acting weird, too. *Am* I getting fired today? What was said about me after I left?

"Oh...yes. Thanks."

"All right. Sorry. I don't mean to make it awkward. I was just checking to make sure you didn't actually quit after everything that happened in the Berkshires. So... glad to hear you're still there, and that's all, really."

This day is getting stranger by the moment. "Did you want to speak to Brick?"

"Yes, but I'll call his cell later. Have a great day, Madi."

"Thanks, Ruby, you, too."

The moment I end the call, Blackthroat's voice comes through on the intercom. "Madison, I need you to call a meeting–" The intercom cuts out, like he took his finger off the button. I lean forward to peer through the window to his office and see him stab the button back down. "Come to my office, Madison."

Again, he has that pissed-as-hell tone, like I've really screwed up, but I can't fathom what it's about. But if I learned one thing over Thanksgiving, it's that he sometimes lashes out *because* he cares. Like his anger over me taking a helicopter in bad weather. And his strained relationship with his mother.

"Of course, sir." I get up from my desk and remember what Aubrey said. Just because I decided I won't have sex with him again doesn't mean I can't torture the guy. I put a little extra swing in my step as I sashay into his office. I'm in a forest green sweater with a criss-cross collar and an opening that frames my decolletage. I wore knee-high boots beneath my pencil skirt. Every day I get better at walking in heels. I stop inside the door and lean my hip against the wall.

"Yes, sir?"

He casts me a dark look, his gaze sweeping up and down my outfit, lingering on the boots, and then on the window to my breasts.

He opens his mouth, but no words come out. Odd for a man who usually cuts right to the point. "Bring me one of those waters," he commands.

I would swear he just came up with that on the spot. Like he wasn't sure why he called me into his office and then made up a reason.

Could it be my boss is as conflicted about what happened between us over the weekend as I am?

"Of course," I say smoothly, pushing off the wall and gliding—as well as I can glide in heels—to the kitchen refrigerator to fetch him the fancy water in a glass bottle that he likes.

When I return, I set it on his desk without opening it. Lord knows, I remember what happened last time when I tried to unscrew it while walking in heels.

Brick draws in a long breath as I stand beside him, his nostrils flaring.

"Anything else?" I breeze, my voice holding the same notes of pleasant attentiveness it held on the day he hired me. As if nothing at all has changed what we are to each other.

The pen between Brick's fingers snaps. Literally snaps. I don't know how that's even possible without using both hands.

It wasn't some plastic Bic pen either. It was one of those sleek metal pens that cost one hundred and twenty-eight dollars. I know because I order them for him.

"Open it," he commands, his voice deep and gruff.

What the hell? Is he just getting off on bossing me around right now? If we were still playing our games, I would be up for it, but I'm too raw from Thanksgiving. From getting close to him, seeing the personal side of him— his family, his wounds—and then getting hustled out the back entrance like the servant that I am. Not hearing a word from him for the rest of the weekend.

I normally pride myself on keeping it together, keeping a facade up when I'm supposed to be professional, but I finally break. After smoothing my walls up all weekend, he just cracked one down again.

"Are you *trying* to get me to quit again?" I snap.

"No!" The word explodes out of him, almost as if he's alarmed.

He snatches my wrist, tugging me closer before releasing it again, as if I scalded him. "No," he repeats. He clears his throat. "Never mind." His tone is back to professional. "You can go."

Oh no. I can't go. Not without actually addressing what's between us. This is too weird.

"Listen, about this weekend—"

Brick's gaze snaps to my face, and I definitely see conflict in his stormy eyes.

19

"Things are getting too... confusing. Or...complicated. I think we should just keep it professional from here on out."

"Right." He looks like he bit into a rotten plum. "I had, uh, concluded the same thing."

I hold my head a little higher. "Good." I point at the water bottle. "So open your own water from now on. We wouldn't want me to reenact my soak and grope from my first week."

Brick chokes on a mirthless laugh. "Maybe that's what I was hoping for." Suddenly he's real again. His shoulders relax, and some of the storm leaves his face. "You got me."

Okay. Cool. I guess he was as conflicted as I was, and I just straightened things out. I toss him a knowing smile as I turn and strut out.

We can do this. We can totally keep things professional.

I feel back on solid ground. Brick just handed me the power by acknowledging he's still attracted to me. Aubrey was right. I can keep up the torture. I have the upper hand here.

I'm not going to lose my head or my heart to my billionaire boss.

Score another one for the assistant.

Chapter Two

B*illy*

I study my alpha during the executive meeting Tuesday.

Brick is in a particular rage today, and I suspect it has everything to do with the fact that he hasn't gotten rid of that uppity human secretary of his.

He's waited too long to find a mate, and now his wolf is hungry for any female–even a human. It's dangerous for an alpha wolf not to mate. A wolf that strong will go nuts without a female if he hasn't mated by mid-life.

He said he would get rid of her, but she's still here.

It makes me want to howl.

We're tossing the racquetball around the room high-speed while we talk–something we started back at Yale as a way to keep our wolves from getting restless when we had to study for finals. We hurl the ball at each other without a pattern, testing our reflexes, trying to get someone to miss.

No one ever does. This is good because at the velocity we throw, we could break a window or put a hole in a wall with it.

I want to study the secretary, but every time I look her way, Brick beans the ball in the direction of my face.

I never thought I'd see my Alpha take his eyes off the prize, distracted by a human no less. His interest in her puts our entire pack in danger.

I never trusted her. She came in here doing and saying everything right.

Red fucking flag.

No one can please Brick. He's a hardass who never stops demanding from his employees and never stops working himself, except to let his wolf off-leash on the weekends to keep from going moon mad. That's what made Moon Co explode into a net worth of eighty-nine billion in the matter of seven years.

She doesn't get ruffled, even when he's particularly dickish. She seems to anticipate exactly what he needs, and she never says anything wrong.

She's too good. Underneath her placid expression, I can sense her mind whirring at high speed, working on multiple fronts at once. My instincts say she has more than one agenda. She has her sights on Brick. Or she's a spy sent from Adalwulf.

I intend to find out.

The ball whizzes around, faster than we've ever volleyed it before, and I finally figure out what has Brick on edge. The secretary leans forward, both her elbows on the table with her forearms pushing her cleavage up, which might not be a big deal, except she's wearing one of those dresses with a cutout over her cleavage, making a perfect window to the curve of her breasts.

I actually hear a snarl from Brick, and he hurls the ball at Nickel without looking away from the secretary's chest.

He's acting protective. Out of control.

Like a wolf in rut.

I bet the little minx loves it.

Nickel hurls the ball at Vance who sends it to me, but the secretary picks that moment to lean forward, probably to give Brick an even better view.

She probably can't even see the ball flying at her head fast enough to give her a black eye, and it's too late–

Except Noah, our spreadsheet guy, heroically throws himself out of his chair to catch the ball just before it smashes into her.

Everyone's looking at the secretary and Noah, but I'm watching Brick. A mixture of relief and anger alternately flicker over his expression.

He settles on anger. "What *in the hell* were you doing?" he demands of Vance, his eyes flashing amber. His wolf is close to the surface. I've never seen him so out of control.

Vance throws his hands up in the air. "Sorry, Madison. I didn't know you were coming in."

Brick turns to Noah and says grimly, "Thank you for saving my assistant from a goddamn concussion."

Noah nods and says something odd– "Always." Not *no problem* or *you're welcome*. Not even *of course*. He says it like a vow, like his job is to protect his alpha's female, and that's when I realize something else.

Noah already knew about Brick's feelings for the secretary. They shared a glance in that exchange that said what happened was meaningful on both sides.

That means any wolf here might know. If it got back to the Adalwulfs, it would be disastrous. I also hate seeing my alpha weakened like this.

We, as his pack brothers, should have insisted more on getting him out to find his fated mate. We should be traveling the world, arranging meetings with every pack princess to find the one female who will trigger the claiming instinct in him.

He's been too focused on growing this company since we left college. On his need and drive to surpass everything Adalwulf Associates is, everything they took from our pack when they murdered Brick's father.

Now he's ensnared by his secretary–a fucking *human*. It's absurd and totally beneath him. Worse–he allowed her to stay overnight at his home–on pack land–and used her to satisfy his sexual needs.

I close my laptop. It's already three o'clock, and we've been in here for hours. I doubt we'll get much more done with the mood Brick's in. "Should we break for the day?"

Brick's still fuming. He glares darkly at Madison's cleavage a moment before he says, "Yes."

Everyone moves at once, like he's the teacher who just released the class, the pent-up tension in the room propelling us out of our chairs and into the elevator. Once I'm inside, I text a team of private investigators I have on standby. They're already on the hunt for every bit of information there is to be had on Madison Evans. We have a few suspicious phone calls to her work phone that might have come from the Adalwulf building, but that's not enough to bring her down. I tell the team to have someone following her at all times, too.

I'll prove she's up to no good. In a choice between his pack or a measly human, Brick will make the right call.

And he'll get rid of her once and for all.

* * *

Brick

"The Benson deal is close to closing. I want everyone in

the legal department in the conference room in five minutes," I snarl through the intercom Wednesday morning.

"They're already on their way," Madison replies calmly. "And your executive team is here."

I've been a holy terror for three days now.

I barely sleep at night. I have to fly back to the Berkshires to run after work and go to the gym in the mornings, but nothing takes the edge off.

Billy and Nickel walk into my office, and Billy surveys me with narrowed eyes.

I rise to my feet, sending my rolling chair backward to hit the bookcase behind my desk. "Don't enter my office without knocking." I blast them both with enough alpha command to make them freeze in their tracks.

"Sorry, Alpha," Billy mutters. "I thought the secre–Madison–told you we were coming in."

Neither of them say a word about the fact that Madison Evans is still in my employ, despite the fact that I said I'd get rid of her.

I can't do it.

It's simply not possible.

I need a steady hit of her scent. Need to see the swish of those hips and the tease of her skin. Getting rid of her is the right move–the only move for my pack–but it doesn't work for me.

I need her here at the office. That's what I keep telling myself. It's about business. She's the best damn assistant I've ever had.

My wolf is confused and thinks she's my mate. I can control that urge.

It would be easier if we hadn't decided to keep things professional, though.

"I'll meet you in the conference room."

I've avoided a private conversation with my executive team all week. Just the sight of them makes me want to throw something. I stride past Billy and Nickel and head to the conference room with them trailing me.

Eagle is already there, directing the in-house legal team.

"Where are we with the updated contract draft?" I demand.

"We have the—" a human starts to explain.

"I wasn't talking to you." I don't even look his way.

"I just gave them the instructions you called in this morning." Eagle reminds me that while I may have called him at six this morning, it's barely past eight still.

I frown at all of them. "Questions? Problems?"

Nobody dares to speak. "I want this done by the end of the day. We'll have lunch brought in. No one leaves this room until I have a completed draft. Understood?"

"What can we do to help?" Nickel asks. He and Billy are standing in the doorway. Billy usually relishes my tirades, but his brows are down today.

He's about to become the subject of my fury.

"*Nothing*. Why are you here? Go back to your offices until I call for you."

"You did call for—"

"Leave it," Nickel mutters, putting a hand on Billy's shoulder to turn him around. The two of them exit.

He's right. I did tell Madison I wanted to see them. I just changed my mind the moment seeing them pissed me off again.

I sweep the room with a challenging gaze, which no one dares to meet. Every employee has their head down over their laptop. Too bad. I was in the mood to fire someone.

I stalk back out, and my cell phone rings. I check the

screen. Seeing it's Ruby, I answer on my way back to my office.

"Brick. I'm just checking in about the Adalwulf Associates board meeting."

Fuck. Like I didn't have enough of my mother with Thanksgiving.

"I'm not going," I say curtly, shutting the door behind me.

Ruby draws a breath. "Really? You're going to tuck your tail and cower in front of our pack rivals?"

She knows exactly how to goad me. A snarl issues from my throat, loud enough that I worry Madison heard it.

Ruby's right, of course. As our mother's heirs, she, Scarlett, and I have seats on the board of Adalwulf and Associates. It was a negotiated part of our parents' mating agreement. Of course, we'll never have a real say in anything discussed there, since we don't hold a majority. So, really, there's no point at all in attending. But Ruby's right. Staying away would make me seem weak.

Ruby continues as if I agreed to go. "I was hoping we could go over together. You, me, and Eagle. I can swing by to pick you two up on the way."

"Fine–but only if we're finished with the Benson deal. When is it?"

"A week from Friday. It's already on your calendar–I checked with Madi yesterday."

I grunt in reply and end the call.

Now I'm really grouchy. There's no way I'm going to be able to work without taking the edge off.

I stare at the wall between my office and Madison as if I could see through it.

I've been calling her into my office for a myriad of inane reasons just to keep her scent here. I can't be certain if it riles me up or takes the edge off. Either way, it's like a drug that I need a constant hit from.

"Madison." I hit the intercom.

She doesn't answer.

I slam my finger down again. "*Madison.*"

My wolf spins and snarls, like a beast in a cage. He's ready to tear the building apart, as if someone kidnapped her. Or–fate forbid–she quit again.

Calm down. I force myself to fill my lungs with air. She's probably in the restroom. She was at her desk when I went by a moment ago.

Still, I find myself stalking through the top floor to make sure. I don't catch her scent near the restrooms, nor is she in the kitchen. I have to loosen my tie because I'm too hot under my collar.

I throw open the conference room door, catching the whites of every employees' eyes before I shut it again.

Not in there.

The elevator dings, and Madison exits in the wool coat I bought her carrying two trays of coffees.

"Where were you?" I demand, even though it's quite obvious. Like the proactive assistant she is, she already gathered drink orders. "You don't pick up their coffee orders."

Madison blinks. "I...do, though."

"No. Just for the executive team. And I don't want you doing that anymore, either. From now on, you'll get them delivered. You don't step away from that desk unless I give you leave." I point at the desk as if I'd grounded her, and she left her room without permission.

I know my behavior's over the top. I'm not sure if I'm subconsciously trying to sabotage our tenuous relationship so she quits again because I can't take this torture, or if I am really this on edge, and I can't dial it back anymore.

Fortunately, Madison keeps her cool. "I'm going to bring these coffees into the conference room, and then I'll come straight to your office." She holds my gaze with those wide, intelligent eyes.

I hesitate. The stormy part of me doesn't want to be mollified, but the eye contact settles my wolf. "Fine." I turn and stalk back to my office.

A moment later, she's in the doorway, pulling off her coat as she enters. "Yes, sir?"

Yes, sir. Yes. Sir. She thinks I want something.

Damn straight I do. I want something from her right here and now.

I frown at her.

"Are you–" she hesitates. "Are you angry that I saw the inner workings of your family? Is that what's bothering you?"

I give her massive points for trying to call me out on my shit.

I get up from the desk and stalk toward her, taking her coat and shutting the door behind her.

"No."

My answer surprises me, but it's true. I'm actually grateful Madison witnessed my family dynamic with the compassion and understanding she brought.

She straightens the skirt on a black peek-a-boo dress with shoulder cutouts. The need to lick the bare skin there makes it hard to think straight.

"Is it the Benson deal?"

"No. Well, partly." I give an impatient wave of my hand and toss her coat onto my chair. I want her scent there when she leaves.

I don't mean to do it. One second she's standing in front of me, the next moment, I have her pinned against the wall, one of my thighs insinuated between her legs, one hand cradling the side of her neck.

Madison gasps and clings to my arms as I shove my nose into her hair and breathe in that delectable scent.

"I'm not supposed to fuck you." My voice is crushed granite.

Madison squirms against me, but not to get away. She rocks her pelvis down over my thigh, rubbing her damp sex against my suit pants.

"You're not..." She sucks in another breath. "Is that what they told you after Thanksgiving? When you were standing out in the snow together?"

I don't know why I'm still surprised by her sharp intelligence.

My teeth scrape along the skin of her neck. "Yes."

She rubs over my thigh, and I grip her ass to help.

"Why? Because I work for you?"

"Yes." My wolf hates the lie, but it's more of a half-truth.

I find the crack of her ass from the back and slide my fingers forward until I hit the damp of her panties.

She grinds harder over my thigh. Her head hits the wall behind her, and she levels another bold gaze at me. "Well, in that case, I'm totally down with screwing the boss."

I study her, taking in the lifted angle of her chin, the fire behind her eyes. Madison Evans doesn't shrink from a fight.

She's alpha female all the way, despite her species, young age, income and class.

"Let's not make it weird, though. Just torrid office sex."

She wants to keep this sex only. *Screwing the boss.*

Okay. Better for me. Downright perfect, in fact.

My wolf disagrees, but I ignore him. I should be glad she wants nothing more than sex.

Thrilled.

It's not like I can mate her.

Fine. Madison has a boss fetish? I'll damn well make every fantasy she has come true. It's an ideal solution. I get what I need–to keep my wolf mollified and be the one who satisfies her–and she gets...well, she gets the orgasms.

"Lock the door."

She fumbles with the lock, then turns, breathless, eyes bright. She definitely has a power exchange fetish. I can work with that. I ignore my wolf, who is pissed that she just wants the fantasy, not me.

I tap the surface of the desk with my index finger. When she arrives, I pick her up and plop her cute ass on it.

She sucks in a breath. I catch the scent of her arousal, and my dick lengthens in my trousers.

"So here's what's going to happen." I stand in front of her, my hands lightly gripping her knees. "Unless I hear you say *no*, I'm going to take what I need, when I need it. Are you down with that?"

Her knees jerk together, but I know it's not to keep me out because a "Yes, sir" tumbles from her pouty lips. *Boss fetish.*

"I need it now." It's no lie. My wolf will go nuts if I don't get inside her again within the hour. I push her knees open and lift them, tipping her back on my desk.

"Oh my *gawd*." She's titillated–or maybe shocked by my behavior.

I can't find it in me to regret any part of it. Not when she's spread out on my desk, her head nearly hanging off the other end, looking so damn appetizing.

"Next time I put you in this position, I'm going to walk around to the other side and use that smart mouth of yours."

Her hardened nipples show through the fabric of her bra and dress.

I slide the pad of my thumb across the satin gusset of her panties. They're already damp, and she makes a needy sound, her inner thighs jerking.

Despite the forcefulness of my initiation, I take my time now, simply stroking over her panties, making sure she warms up.

"You want my mouth here?" I meet her gaze.

She's holding her breath, watching me. She nods.

I go slowly, lifting her knees up as I lower my head between them. I pull her panties to the side with my teeth, then lick into her.

She gasps, her inner thighs slapping my shoulders. I screw one finger inside her as I flick her clit with my tongue. "Yes, please," she whispers.

It's cute as hell.

I shouldn't be so enamored with this girl, but everything she does, everything she says, everything she is seems to affect me.

The need to satisfy her overrides my need to claim her. I pull her panties off and work a second finger into her tight channel, then use both fingers to stroke her inner wall.

She thrashes her legs, her high heels kicking my back and ribs as I make her squirm. I rise, resting my thumb over her clit and pumping the two fingers in and out while I study her face. "You gonna come on my fingers, little girl?"

She's breathing hard, that open window on her dress showing her chest heaving. "I don't...answer...to that."

I find her G-spot and fuck it, my fingertips nailing it everytime I stroke in.

Her hips grind and buck beneath me.

"I don't...Stop."

I go still. Well, I stop finger-fucking her. I can't prevent my thumb from lightly rubbing over her clit.

"Please." She sounds so unlike herself, but then she's on the edge of an orgasm. At least, I thought she was.

I slide my fingers out. "What do you need, Windows?" My voice is as rough as sandpaper.

Her lids droop. "You. I mean, not your fingers." A blush spreads over her face and across the open window to the skin at her chest.

A smug smile twists my lips. "You want my cock, Madison?"

"Uh huh."

I unzip my pants and fist my erection. "You say a lot of things with that sassy mouth of yours. Don't tell me you can't ask for what you need."

I reach in my pocket for a condom and frown when I find none. I tossed them when I committed to keeping my hands off my sexy secretary.

She sees my frown and interprets it correctly. "It's okay," she calls. "I'm on the pill."

My cock jumps in my fist. She wants me inside her, bare? My control's about to shatter, but I force myself to check. "You're sure."

She nods slowly, staring at my dick. Her tongue touches her perfect lips, and my cock swells to an impossible size.

"Say it."

Of course, my little alpha female assistant can never back down from a challenge. She pushes up on her forearms and meets my gaze squarely. "Give me. Your cock."

I laugh. An actual laugh. I *love* her getting sexually aggressive with me.

"My pleasure."

I drag the head of my cock through her juices, teasing her before I part her sweet flesh and feed her my length.

She watches the place where our bodies connect, I watch her lovely face.

I've never been so fascinated by a female in my life. Her every expression, every nuance captivates me. I thought fucking the assistant would get her out of my system, but it seems to be the opposite. The more times I have her, the more I need her.

She's becoming an addiction, and I'm afraid I'll never satisfy the craving.

I'm careful, giving her time to get used to my size. I was too rough last time, and I have to remember she's human. But as her scent curls around me, as her hot, sweet flesh engulfs my cock, I grip her thighs tighter, push in with more force.

Her soft moan of approval drives me insane. Before I know it, I'm pounding into her, shaking the desk with the force of my thrusts, making her cover her mouth to muffle her cries.

I bring my thumb back to that sensitive nubbin at the apex of her sex and give it a rough rub as I jackhammer into her.

She screams behind her palm, hips jacking up off the desk. Even though I want to go on forever like this with her, I can't. Not when her hot flesh seizes around my cock.

I growl, eyes rolling up to my brows as my climax comes on like a bullet train. I slap against her ass with my loins driving to the finish. Heat makes me want to shred out of my suit like a werewolf caught in a shift before he can undress. I slam in deep and come, my thighs jerking against the desk, my thumb still rubbing her swollen clit. She comes some more, even harder this time, her internal muscles spasming around my dick, dragging me halfway to heaven.

I take a moment to breathe. Let the tilting floor right itself. My vision returns to normal.

I grab a couple tissues from the box on my desk and use them to clean us both.

Madison sits, a lovely flush making her skin glow.

I purposely play the part of the dick, since that's what she seems to want. "I need the paperwork from the Adirondack purchase on my desk in five. Tell Noah I need to see him at nine thirty, and let HR know about your salary increase."

Her eyes flick down in an uncharacteristic gesture before they return to my face. "Actually, I've reconsidered my salary request." Her voice is polite and businesslike as always. "It was excessive and made in a moment of anger."

I study her, trying to understand her change of heart on this one. I did notice she didn't seem glad when she won the negotiation. Perhaps she doesn't feel she truly earned it.

She slides her butt toward the edge of the desk, but I don't move to let her hop down. "Besides, I don't want people thinking I got it because I'm screwing the boss."

I narrow my eyes, not liking the way this is going. "Am I paying you for sex, Madison?"

"No." She says it so immediately that I believe her. Her flush deepens. "That's what I mean. I don't want it to feel that way."

"You negotiated a salary I'm willing to pay." I step back, so she can stand while we discuss her livelihood. "There's no reason to back down from that."

"No, I'm good." She hops down and straightens her dress. "I already have that paperwork ready for you."

Of course she does.

I walk around to sit behind my desk, glorying in the fact

that it's now covered in her scent. That she's covered in mine.

I didn't like that hint of defeat around her with the salary thing, though. Madison is the type of person who likes to win. For whatever reason, I enjoy watching her win, even against me. So her backing down doesn't feel right.

But I understand her concern. Genevieve, my HR Director, would've shit a brick at the new salary, which is close to her own.

I pick up the office phone and call Genevieve.

She answers smoothly. "Good morning, Mr. Blackthroat. What can I do for you?"

"Send a fifty thousand dollar bonus to my assistant, Madison, payable today."

Genevieve chokes and sputters a little. "A-absolutely, sir."

I ordinarily wouldn't bother to explain myself, but since Madison is sensitive to people thinking she got a raise because I got into her panties, I say, "She gave up her Thanksgiving holiday and risked her life to make sure an important deal closed, and I want her properly rewarded."

"That's...um. Okay. Yes, absolutely. I'm sorry I couldn't give her your executive team's personal phone numbers on Wednesday, but I did try to reach them personally."

Ah. Part of me wants to rip her a new one for blocking Madison from getting things done, but Genevieve was just doing her job. Protecting the personal information of my team is important. "You did the right thing. Madison just went above and beyond." I hang up, so I don't have to hear whatever simpering reply she has.

Madison taps on the door and walks in with a sheaf of papers. "Here are the closing documents. Noah will be here, as requested."

"Thank you, Madison." Our eyes meet as I take the papers, and she sucks in a breath, as if the contact shocked her. Or maybe it was just my thanks. It's hard not to be grateful after she just offered her hot little body up to me like that.

Even if she is a hard-to-decode human with a smart mouth and a reluctance to get personal.

Not that I was trying to get personal.

Not at all.

Our *just sex* arrangement is going to work out perfectly for me. My wolf will stay calm, and I won't have to figure out what to do about her, beyond being her boss with benefits.

Even so, something about it doesn't sit right with me. But maybe that's just my ego. I'm used to women throwing themselves at me, trying to entrap me in a permanent relationship. Maybe my pride can't take it when the first one I can stand for longer than one night doesn't show any interest in snaring me.

Madi

"Goodnight, Jerry," I call to the janitor as I leave for the day.

He's wearing earbuds, but he must not listen to his music too loudly because he always seems to hear me. He lifts a hand. "Have a good night, Madi."

Blackthroat offered me a ride home when he left a half an hour ago, but I refused. Things are already weird enough. I don't need him driving me home like we're dating.

Instead, Tony's waiting for me when I exit the building. He smiles as I reluctantly trudge to him. It's weird to be escorted to and from work in luxury like this, but Tony's just trying to do his job.

I have him drop me off a block away from my apartment, so I can pick up an order of gluten free eggplant lasagna from my favorite Italian restaurant.

While I'm waiting for my food, I call Aubrey to check in. "Are you at home?"

"I get off in an hour. What's up? How was torturing the boss?"

"Um... yeah. I slept with him again. Only there was no sleeping involved."

"Ooh, scandalous! What *was* involved?"

"The surface of a very large desk." Heat licks between my legs remembering it all. "I didn't mean to. But he was all grumpy, and then he confessed that the dude-bros said he's not supposed to sleep with me anymore, so I had to meet that challenge."

"Whaaaat? Oh damn, I think he really likes you."

"Well, he can't," I say firmly, pacing in front of the Italian restaurant. "I've already thought this through. There's only one way this can go, as I told him when he brought the coffee."

"And what way is that?" I hear Aubrey bracing against whatever she's expecting to come out of my mouth.

"It has to stay in fantasy-land."

"Excuse me?"

"The *screwing the boss* fantasy. Or *screwing the secretary* for him."

There's a businessman who must also be waiting for his to-go order standing nearby. He looks over like I've caught his attention. I ignore him.

"Mads, I'm sure this all makes perfect sense in your head, but I'm not following."

"It can't go beyond that."

"Because...?"

"Because I already got too close to him over Thanksgiving. I met his mom and his niece and nephew, and Aubrey, he is an adorable uncle. Seeing him with kids made my ovaries ache."

"And you don't want to want him." Aubrey finally catches on.

"Exactly." I throw my hand in the air.

The businessman looks over again.

"Also"--I turn my back on the businessman and walk away, hunching over to speak more privately-- "Things are super hot right now, and part of what makes it hot is the fact that he's the boss."

"Ah, that's the fantasy you mentioned." I strain to hear Aubrey over the noise of a rowdy party of four exiting the restaurant.

"Yes! Wait, hang on a minute." A waitress comes over with my bag, and I thank her and head off down the dark sidewalk towards home. "I just want to keep it in that realm, so it will stay exciting. If he takes me to lunch and I relax around him, then it won't be nearly so fun and naughty to do it over the desk, you know what I mean?" I mumble the words *do it over the desk,* so people walking near me won't be subjected to my sexcapades without consent.

"So basically, you're into the power dynamic. You know you can keep a power exchange in a relationship as an agreed upon thing."

"I don't know..."

"What's the real hang-up here?"

"I just want to keep it low key. I'm afraid if I'm actually his girlfriend, I might lose interest."

"Is that it? Or are you afraid you're going to fall for a

billionaire who will knock you up and bail, just like your dad did?"

"Well, I'm on the pill."

"You know what I mean." Aubrey's giving me the straight-talk right now, and I sort of hate her for it.

"Do you think I'm just letting myself be used?" I change tack again. I'm admittedly all over the place with this situation. "Am I disrespecting myself by screwing the boss?"

"Now you're just being absurd. That is the most sex-negative, slut-shaming, stupid thing you've ever said. Do you love the sex?"

My knees go weak remembering Blackthroat's large hands picking me up by the waist and sitting me on his desk. *From now on, I'll take what I need, when I need it. And I need it now.*

Who says that? And how interesting that he chose the word *need* and not *want.*

"Yes."

"But sex is just for his enjoyment, right? And women should withhold it from men to be respectable?" Sarcasm drips from her voice.

I laugh when I hear how absurd it is.

"What, are you catering to the patriarchy now that you work with them?"

"Okay, you're right. That was the dumbest thing I've ever said."

"Literally."

"You got lasagna again, right?"

"You know it. Extra garlic bread for you."

"You're the best."

"I know. I'll see you soon."

I end the call and hustle up the stairs to our apartment.

Ugh. I still don't know where I am with all this. Aubrey

couldn't have been encouraging me to have a real relationship with Blackthroat could she?

No, she was just calling me on my shit, so I couldn't lie to myself about my real hangups. That doesn't mean those hangups aren't legit.

Chapter Three

Brick

"Where are we with the contract?" I demand. It's Sunday evening, and I'm ready to shred the walls of my office. I've kept the legal and analyst teams in my conference room for five days, which means working through the weekend.

Closing on the Benson deal isn't just a four hundred and forty million dollar benefit to MoonCo, it's a victory over the Adalwulfs.

"Three hours more, max," Eagle says. He looks as haggard as everyone in the room. None of us have had more than a few hours' sleep in days.

"I'll order in more food," Madi says in that smooth, capable voice that gets my dick harder than stone.

I have to lock my jaw to keep the growl of desire from issuing from my throat.

The punishing hours I inflicted on my employees have been even worse for me. Not getting out to run my wolf in the Berkshires or even to spar with Darius at the gym has left me even more out of control than I was going into this week.

Even if I was the kind of dick to leave his team working late hours while out enjoying myself, I'm now incapable of leaving the building while Madi is still in it. And she refuses to leave until I've dismissed the team each night.

The only thing that takes the edge off is ordering her into my office and locking the door. Getting her on my desk or against a wall.

My executive team is pissed at me for not getting rid of her. I don't give a fuck. She is necessary to the Moon Co operations. That's what I keep telling myself.

It's not like I'm going to mate her. Even if I wanted to, I can't. The destruction that would bring on the pack, the danger that would put all of us in make it impossible.

Forty-five minutes later, Madison enters the conference room pushing a catering cart.

"Thank God it's not more pizza or sandwiches," one of the analysts mutters.

Madison sets out the aluminum catering trays.

"Smells delicious. What is it?" Another one gets up to help her, which makes me want to tear out his throat.

"Thank you. I thought since we're so close, you deserved a real dinner tonight." She uncovers two of the trays at once.

Eagle chokes on the Perrier he was drinking. It's trays of...*steak and lobster?*

My naughty, naughty assistant. Is she trying to earn a reprimand?

"Thank you," Noah says, and I have to rip my collar open. *Did she order this banquet for him?*

Madison smiles at him and signs something. My wolf goes ape-shit.

44

He chuckles, signing in return, but when he darts a look at me and sees my murderous expression, his smile vanishes, and his gaze snaps to his laptop.

I force myself to wait until Madi finishes unloading the cart, then I walk out of the room. "In my office," I say in a low voice as I pass by her.

"Of course, Mr. Blackthroat," she intones.

I'm almost blinded by jealousy, but I somehow make it to my office. The moment she enters, I lock the door and pin her against it.

"What did you say to him?" I growl.

Her eyes widen with genuine surprise. "What?"

"To Noah. What did you say?"

Two bright spots of color appear on her cheeks, and her brows drop, but characteristically, she smooths her face and adopts a professional tone. "I said we may as well eat well if the Big Bad Boss is keeping us here all weekend. It was a joke. I'm sorry."

"You don't sign to him again. I don't want you flirting—"

"Flirting? Are you nuts?" she breaks character, her real irritation showing through now.

"New rule—don't talk to him again. You work for me. Was that food for him?" I'm being irrational. I'm totally out of control, but I can't seem to dial back my possessiveness.

Madi stares at me, eyes wide. "You're jealous?"

I stare back. Having Madison's body up against mine soothes my wolf. Her scent evens my heartbeats. My brain starts to come back on line.

"Wow, Big Bad. That's totally inappropriate but, um, kind of hot."

"Was the food for *me* or for *him*?"

Madi's lips purse together in a sassy pucker. "I may

have been pushing the envelope a bit to see what my big bad boss would do."

My aggression instantly drops, morphing into something more suave. More nuanced. Much hotter.

Madison wasn't flirting with Noah.

She was flirting with me.

If she wants to make this part of her boss fetish, I can one hundred percent go with it.

Recovering some of my control, I ease back and clear my throat. "Did you get approval for that expenditure first, Ms. Evans?"

She bats her eyes at me. "No, sir."

"Come here." I take her hand and lead her to my desk, then sweep my arm across the surface to clear it. "Bend over, Ms. Evans. You've earned a reprimand."

She lets out a breathy sound of excitement as I push her torso down over the desk and jerk her hips to straighten her out. I deliver three sharp spanks to one side of her ass, then three to the other.

"Ooh, ow!"

I stop and rub away the sting. "Too hard?" I murmur, leaning over to speak in her ear like we're on stage and this is an aside.

"Um, a little."

The scent of her arousal curls in my nostrils. I keep rubbing out the sting, dragging the skirt of her peek-a-boo dress higher with each glorious stroke.

"I think I need to spank you with your panties down tonight," I tell her, my balls drawing up with the excitement of seeing her bare ass.

She's wearing black thigh-highs and a lacy black thong that I instantly decide I'm going to keep. For now, though, I slide it down to just above the thigh-highs, making a pretty frame out of my target. My handprints stand out on her pale skin.

Yes. More. Mark her, my wolf growls.

I don't slap her again, though. Not right away. Instead, I slide my fingers between her legs. She's slick, her flesh plumped with blood flow, her opening parted for me. I slip two fingers inside her, and she moans, loudly.

"Quiet," I order. It may be more exciting to get nailed by the boss when there is a conference room full of employees down the hall, but there's no way in hell I'd actually let any of them know what's going on in here.

Nickel and Noah will probably catch the scent of it, but they both already know something's going on between us.

Madison claps a hand over her own mouth.

"That's right. I want all those moans muffled, Ms. Evans. Show me you can obey orders."

She soaks my fingers.

I slide them out and suck her juices from my skin. Satisfaction starts to seep in through the cracks in my sanity. This–these moments–make it all worth it.

Keeping Madison in my employ. Torturing myself on a daily basis. It's all for this.

"Now hold still for your spanking." I give her a slap– lighter this time. "When you use the company credit card" –I deliver a spank to her other cheek– "for a five thousand dollar meal" –another spank.

"It was less than two thousand," Madison interjects.

My lips tug, but I deliver a harder spank. "For *any* extravagant meal" –two more spanks– "I require prior approval."

She reaches back to cover her ass, so I pin her wrist to her lower back and rub her reddened cheeks.

"Good girl. You took your punishment well. Time for a

reward." I tug her panties off over her heels and tuck them in my pocket.

I forget to modulate my strength when I lift her hips straight in the air to drop her to her hands and knees on my giant walnut desk.

She gasps, startled by the move. I hook my thumbs at the base of her asscheeks where they meet her thigh and pull her open to reveal her glistening sex.

"Go down on your forearms," I order.

She obeys, lifting her pretty pink core to me further. I take full advantage of the position, licking into her. I suck and nibble at her labia, trace inside with the tip of my tongue.

Her muffled moans grow more frantic.

I find her clit with my fingertip while I penetrate her with my tongue, then use my fingers inside her for more oomph. I alternate fucking her with my fingers and sliding up to rub her clit, driving her into a dripping frenzy.

"Come for me, Madi," I order, my voice rough with need.

She reaches back and rubs her own clit as she comes around my fingers. I leave them inside her, slowly circling the raised stiffened tissue of her G-spot with my fingertips.

"Oh my gawd," she moans.

"Oh, I'm not finished with you, yet, Ms. Evans."

* * *

Madi

Brick eases his fingers from my channel and lifts me off the desk. Damn, that man is strong. Those muscles built from all that running and working out at the gym apparently aren't just for show.

He holds me up by the elbow when I wobble on my feet. My limbs aren't working yet. I'm still dizzy from the incredible orgasm. Still drunk on my boss' pheromones and commanding touch.

"Show me your best work." He says in that gruff, demanding voice, lowering his gaze to the floor and unbuckling his belt.

Understanding his meaning, I drop to my knees and unbutton his pants. His erection springs out, thick and long. The tip is already weeping.

"Mmm, this looks painful, sir." I flick my tongue over the slit to taste his essence. "Let me take care of it for you."

I never thought of myself as a sex kitten, but Brick Blackthroat has turned me into one. For the first time in my life, I'm not just the nerdy kid trying to pretend she isn't lower middle class. I'm someone highly desirable. Someone who incites extreme levels of jealousy and desire.

It's hard to believe, but here we are, having crazy, frantic sex while the rest of the company works on the most important merger of the decade.

I slide my mouth over his length, loving the way he sucks in his breath over his teeth.

"That's it, Ms. Evans." His large hand cups the back of my head, guiding me forward and back. "I expect the utmost professionalism from you."

My lips quirk around his cock, but he cuts in with a sharp reprimand.

"No. This is serious. I need this cock sucked hard right now, Ms. Evans."

I hollow my cheeks and suck hard as I pull away.

"That's right. Now lick my balls."

I fist his cock and hold it to the side to bring my tongue

to his balls. I trace between them with my tongue, then suck one into my mouth.

"Good girl," Brick chokes. "Very good, Madison."

I suck the other ball then bring the head of his cock into my mouth, keeping my fist around the base. I bob my head over his length, pulling my fist at the same time, to simulate the feeling of me taking his entire cock into my mouth– which would be impossible. As I suck, I cradle his balls in my hand, lightly stroking the textured skin with my thumb.

Brick's belly shudders in and out. His balls lift. I suck faster, lifting my gaze to his face.

"Oh, that's so hot, Madi."

This undoes me. When he calls me Madi. When the pretense of boss/employee gets dropped for a moment, and it's like we're something more.

It scares the hell out of me.

I'm in danger of falling head over heels in love with this man, and I don't want to lose control like that. I know it would end in disaster.

I pop off and put things back into role play. "Is this how you like it, Mr. Blackthroat?"

Brick's eyes gleam unnaturally bright as he catches me under the armpits and lifts me all the way off the floor and onto his desk. "Take notes, Madi," he growls as he spreads my knees wide. "This is how I like it done." He shoves into me.

I cry out, and he covers my mouth. There's no more foreplay. No more finesse. Brick Blackthroat is an animal now, going at it with a feral need.

I start to quake with an impending orgasm immediately. The level of passion between us is beyond what I ever believed possible. Blackthroat fucks me like his company depends on it. Like his life depends on it. Like this is a race he not only intends to finish, he intends to dominate. To win.

And he has won. It's hard for me to imagine I could ever have sex this good with anyone else. It's hard to imagine ever willingly walking away from anything this man offers– even if it's just the scraps of a torrid office affair.

"Come for me, Madi." His voice is pure gravel. He thrusts in hard, holding the fronts of my thighs to keep me from sliding away. "Come for me...right...now!"

He thrusts in, his face contorting with his release.

I wrap my legs behind his waist and hold him in against me, coming and coming right along with him.

For a long moment, we just pant together, our breath synchronized like a heartbeat. Then Brick eases out. "Did you get all that, Ms. Evans?" His lips quirk up in an uncharacteristic smile that makes my heart flop helplessly in my chest.

"Yes, sir." I sound breathless.

He hands me a few tissues as he disposes of the condom.

I hop off the desk, but he picks me up and places me back there. "I didn't say I was through with you." His voice is softer now, the strain of the grueling week absent after the release. He brushes my hair out of my face and kisses my forehead. "Go get yourself some steak and lobster and then go home," he murmurs. "They're almost done."

I try not to melt. "I'm not leaving until the project is done. I'm part of the team." My stomach growls. "But I won't pass on dinner. Shall I bring you a plate?"

His expression softens even more. "I'll come with you."

I absolutely hate the way my heart flip flops in my chest as we walk out of his office together.

Chapter Four

rick

By Monday night, I'm back from California, with the deal closed, and my nose in the snow.

I race at full speed in the darkness, narrowly dodging trees like I'm in some kind of competition. Letting my wolf off-leash in the Berkshires after being pent up half the week is a relief, as is having the Benson deal closed.

I should be out celebrating with my team. Opening thousand dollar bottles of champagne and eating at the best restaurant in Manhattan.

Instead, I'm alone in the woods.

I took Eagle with me to close the deal instead of Billy or Nickel, which I'm sure pissed them off. I just wasn't willing to sit in the private jet with them and field their questions or judgements about what I'm doing or not doing with Madi.

Eagle already knows exactly what I've been doing with Madi, and he also knew better than to mention it on the trip.

When I get back to the manse, I shower and flop down on the bed Madi slept in. Of course, Liz has washed the sheets and aired out the room, but I was still drawn to the far wing of the mansion, like my subconscious–or my wolf–wants me to remember what happened there.

I know this is more than screwing the secretary.

Far more.

Everyone who was here that day knew it when I nearly went nuts about her disappearance.

Madi is my mate.

I stare at the empty place beside me and try to remember how it felt to spoon her cold body. That gnawing fear still in my throat that she wouldn't be all right. Or that she would really quit on me.

My phone rings, and I lunge for it, even though Madi wouldn't dare call me after hours. Not unless I called her first.

It's Eagle. What in the fuck could he want? We just parted in Manhattan a few hours ago. It can't be something to do with the deal–it closed.

It better not be.

I swipe right. "Eagle. What is it?"

"Everything's fine. I came into the office to get the paperwork filed with the SEC."

"Okay." I bite back my impatience. The run took the edge off, but thinking about Madi brought it back.

"Did you give the whole legal and analyst team the whole week off?"

"What?"

"So you didn't."

"What are you talking about?"

"I was looking for my team, and every single one of them were gone. When I called HR, Genevieve said you told them all to take the week off for a job well done."

An involuntary smile starts to tug at my lips.

My naughty, naughty secretary.

Someone is looking for another reprimand.

"I see. Is Madi at work, or did she give herself the week off, too?"

"Ah." Eagle goes silent as he no doubt realizes he's in the middle of a lovers' stand-off. He clears his throat. "I don't know. Is this a problem I need to address?"

"No. I'll address it. Can you get the filing done without your team?"

"Yes, it's fine. I'll handle it personally. I would have anyway."

"Good."

I end the call and dial my office number.

"Mr. Blackthroat."

"You're still at work."

"Yes, sir. I had a million things to catch up on that I couldn't get to last week while we were finishing the Benson deal. How did it go?"

There's a warmth in the center of my chest I try to ignore. It's one thing to have my wolf attracted to Madi. It's another to admire her brilliant mind and extreme capability.

It's something completely different to feel true affection blooming. Pleasure at the way she asks how it went– like she's a true partner to me, not just an employee I like to fuck. I suddenly want to be near her not just to ravish that hot little body again but just to be near her. To catch one of her off-hand gestures, like tucking that sleek bob behind one ear or the impudent tilt of her chin when challenged.

"So the Big Bad Boss didn't give *you* the week off for a job well done, as well?"

"No, he didn't. Mainly because I wanted to be around when he found out he'd given those orders."

"Mmm hmm. How do you think he'll react to your abuse of his authority?"

Her voice gets husky. "Well, I'm expecting he'll give me a *personal taste* of that authority."

"Oh you can count on it, Ms. Evans. He is not pleased that Eagle has to file with the SEC without a single member of his team available to support him."

Madi draws in an audible breath. "I'm so sorry." All innuendo is gone from her voice, and I'm instantly sorry I gave her a real reason for regret.

"It's all right. He can handle it. And I can handle you. Expect punishment tomorrow."

"I'm sorry about Eagle's team. I can contact Genevieve and—"

"No," I cut her off. "I said it's handled. We'll discuss the situation *thoroughly* tomorrow. Understand?"

"I went too far."

"No. Keep testing me, Madi. I like it."

Chapter Five

M*adi*

The next morning, I have a smirk on my face when Tony comes to pick me up in the limo. My vanilla latte is waiting for me, and the first sip is enough to prime me for a fantastic morning.

Expect punishment tomorrow. I wriggle in my seat. Under my work dress, my sex is warm and wet, imagining what delicious torment my boss has imagined for me today.

Tony crosses the Brooklyn Bridge, but when the time comes to take the turn towards the financial district, he takes a left towards the docks instead.

I lean forward to catch his attention. "We're not going to the office?"

"No, Ms. Evans, I was ordered to bring you here."

I check my calendar. A notification has popped up, alerting me that my day is blocked off for one long appointment. I click to find more details, and there are none.

Tony pulls up to a helicopter pad and escorts me to the pilot, who guides me towards the waiting chopper.

"This way, Ms. Evans." He helps me into my seat and straps me in.

I expect him to wait for Brick to join me, but in a few minutes, we're airborne. The last time I was in a helicopter, I was coming back from Berkshires. Is that where we're going? My calendar and email don't give me any clues.

I guess not knowing is part of my punishment.

We fly over the Hudson river and leave the city behind. I work as best as I can on my tablet, but as we approach what looks like the thick, wooded area of upper state New York, my trepidation grows. Am I being flown out to the Blackthroat residence again? Will Brick's family be there? It's a workday, and I can't imagine why I'd be needed there.

I was looking forward to my punishment, but that would be real torture.

My tension grows as the helicopter approaches a gorgeous Tudor style mansion on a hilltop. Built of light brown brick, it looks similar to the Blackthroat ancestral home. Just past it are several long low white buildings arranged around a bright blue outdoor pool. From above the whole place looks like a fine estate, complete with gardens and patios and winding rock pathways that connect everything.

We land some distance away, on a blue slab of pavement bound by a lush green field. I wait for the pilot to help me out, and he points me to the edge of the helicopter pad where a white woman in a purple-gray smock waves to me.

"Welcome to Miravelle Resort," she greets me. She's holding a binder and makes no move to shake my hand. "I'm Jennifer, and I'll be your spa attendant today. How was your flight?"

Spa attendant?

"Fast," I say. Before I can ask what's going on, she beams and says, "Right this way."

I follow her down the pea-gravel path toward one of the white buildings. Even in the dead of winter, the land-scaping is immaculate, with elegant white birch trees rising over a carpet of purple heather and evergreen shrubs. "This is a spa?"

"And a wellness resort." She hurries ahead to open a door for me revealing an inner walkway lined with indoor fountains and shining geode crystals larger than me. I want to stand and gape, but for Jennifer's sake, I hustle through. It's chilly today, with snow on the ground, and she's not wearing a coat. Her round cheeks are pink with cold.

I check my phone again. "Is there a meeting here or...?"

"Oh no." She opens the next set of doors and sweeps out a hand. "Your boss booked the whole spa for you today. You're getting a sampling of all our top treatments." She flips open the binder and shows me my itinerary, starting with a body wrap and facial, and ending with a massage and relaxation time in the saunas and serenity pool. I'm grateful she's so excited to explain all this because I'm still in shock. I expected Brick to dish out something awful and epic, but I never expected this.

Tears smart my eyes. "My boss booked all of this...for me?" Oh God, what is happening?

"Yes." Jennifer closes the binder with a snap and hugs it to her ample chest. "He said you've been working hard on a project and deserve it."

"He said that?"

"Well, it was implied." Her eyes take a dreamy cast. "You're so lucky to work for him. He sounds like the greatest boss ever. So generous."

"He's....something, all right." My chest is unaccountably tight. My eyes are still smarting.

I don't understand what's happening right now. I pushed the envelope by giving everyone the week off, recklessly testing my boss. The moment I heard my actions had caused a real dilemma, I regretted them. It's completely unlike me to make a rash or impractical decision. Especially one that would result in my punishment.

Clearly, I'm losing sight of what's at all within the bounds of appropriateness at work.

But I expected more punishment or funishment at best. Maybe I was testing my unfireability. Possibly, I was subconsciously *trying* to get fired to end this relationship before it destroys me.

I never expected a lavish reward like this. I expected more tit for tat. I misbehaved. I thought there might be a sexy reprimand. This? This feels too much like a reward.

Or worse–unthinkable–too much like a relationship.

Things are definitely getting out of hand.

Jennifer takes my coat and gets me a cup of tea to enjoy while she gives me a tour of the spa amenities. In the empty dressing room, she lays out a spa robe and flip flops for me to change into.

A few hours later, I'm buffed and polished and limp. A massage therapist has squeezed all the tension from my neck and shoulders.

I'm drifting on a purple-gray lounger in the relaxation room when Jennifer reappears with another cup of herbal tea.

"How was the massage?"

"Blissful." I stretch like I've just woken up.

"You're welcome to nap here or try the pool. We have a few bathing suits in our shop, if you'd like to try them. Or we have this selection of lounge wear if you prefer." She holds up a hanger holding a soft-looking pair of flowy white pants, paired with a silky gown covered in a gorgeous print of flowers and peacocks. A tag flutters out of the sleeve, and my eyes pop at the price.

"Oh, it's all complimentary," she says, reading my expression correctly. "You have a shop credit as well."

I have to hand it to Brick. When he does something, he goes all in.

"Well, in that case, I'll take that outfit. And a bathing suit."

The indoor-outdoor pool area is just as luxurious as the rest of the spa. I float in the heated water, even venturing a brief swim outside to watch the steam shimmer between me and the snow banks.

I end up back in the dimly lit relaxation room, dozing to the sound of running water. There are loungers for thirty people, but I'm the only one here.

My phone is silenced in my locker, but I'm tempted to text Brick and tease him about finally taking the time to show his employees he appreciates them.

Except I shouldn't be here. I can't encourage this sort of behavior. It's above and beyond what a Big Bad Boss would do. I told myself I wouldn't catch feelings for Brick. I'm just using him.

As soon as I curl up under the fluffy spa blanket and close my eyes for a nap, my brain conjures up a fantasy of Brick.

He's been using me for sex every day, and my body is primed for it. I can smell his woodsy cologne and imagine him leaning over me. Dark and handsome, he'd glower at everything in this room as if it offended him. And he'd turn that delicious glare on me...

"Dreaming of me?" he growls above me.

I smile, still caught in my fantasy, when a large hand clamps on my foot where it's slipped from the blanket.

Instead of freaking out, I inhale more of his wild scent and open my eyes. Brick looms over me, his face in shadow.

I knew it was him.

"Mr. Blackthroat." I smile. "Are you here for a massage?"

Even in the dark room, I can see his flat expression. But he settles on the edge of my lounger, still holding my foot captive, so I decide to tease him. "Or are you here to order me to relax?"

"If I did, would you obey?"

"Mmm, depends on what mood I'm in."

"You've been particularly impertinent these last few weeks."

Oh here it is. The *punish the naughty secretary* game he promised. My favorite game. This is safe territory for us.

"You love it. You rewarded me with a whole spa day." I wave at the trickling fountain. "If this is punishment, I'd like more. A lot more."

"Oh you'll get more." He leans closer, sliding his hand up my bare leg. This is more like it.

"But really, this was too much."

"Well, I need my assistant in top shape, so I can work her harder."

My sex clenches. "You do work me hard."

"So hard."

I stretch out, still feeling languid from my day of relaxation. The blanket flops to the ground, giving him a full view of me in my new bathing suit. The bikini is a little smaller than what I'd normally wear, and when I move, the thin strip of fabric between my legs slips, giving him a peek of my pussy.

His eyes gleam in the dark.

I move my foot, so it's propped on his thigh. I can't believe I'm being so bold. Lemongrass tea must make me shameless. "Maybe you need a day of relaxation."

"Lying around isn't my style. I prefer something more... vigorous." And he reaches out and tugs the string of my bikini top, making my breasts pop out of the triangles. My nipples harden as they're exposed to the air. My abs tighten, and my core begins to throb.

"Why Mr. Blackthroat," –I make my voice high and breathy– "whatever do you mean?"

"Let me show you." With his hands on my calves, he slides me down, so I'm flat on my back. He climbs over me, planting his hands by my shoulders and moving so his big body hovers over mine. Up close, I can see his hair is tousled, unruly. I reach up to smooth it, and he catches my wrist, pinning it beside my head.

Now I'm panting. His fingers are rough on my bare skin as he skims his free hand down my side, leaving a trail of goosebumps in its wake.

He's drinking in the sight of me half naked. "This is hardly appropriate work attire, Ms. Evans."

"No? I kind of like it." I wriggle my hips, and the bikini bottoms slide over my slick labia.

"You better not wear it in front of anyone but me." His possessive stare takes my breath away. "Or else."

"Or else...what?"

His growl makes me shiver. He reaches down and fists the bikini bottoms, tugging them so they're tight between my pussy lips. He pulls harder, flossing the fabric against my clit. I writhe, and he drops his chest, pinning my upper torso while still keeping his full weight off me. He watches my face closely as he works the bathing suit like a rope between my legs. It's perfect and painful, and he knows just how to twist the cloth to torture me. In the dim light, his eyes seem to glow.

The stimulation makes me writhe under him. I rock from side to side, but there's no escape, just the friction of my bare breasts against the expensive Italian cotton of his shirt.

"Oh, fuck." My orgasm is there, just out of reach. My chest is flushing, my breasts growing hot and tight.

"I don't know if you deserve to come," he taunts. "You've been so bad."

If I don't come soon I'll die. "Oh my God, please..."

Light flares in his eyes, and he rips the bathing suit off. I cry out, wanting more, and then his mouth is on me. His beard is rough on my sensitive skin, and the discomfort combined with his lush tongue pushes me over.

My orgasm wrenches me in half, but I don't have time to recover before he's on me, wrenching open his pants, so he can thrust inside me. The stretch makes me gasp—he's so big, it takes me a moment to adjust, but I'm sopping wet, and in no time, he's driving into me, rooting so deep I can feel him in my throat.

Orgasm after orgasm rips through me, one rolling into the next until I'm shuddering nonstop. And still Brick rocks into me. The lounger cushions slide sideways off the frame, and we both go with it. We land on the floor, and he just flips me over to hands and knees, and keeps fucking me senseless. I push back against him until I'm too limp to hold myself up. He pulls me up by my hair and grinds against my bottom, filling me with his cum.

I'm out of breath like I've run up ten flights of stairs. My throat is hoarse, my cries ringing in my ears.

And I'm boneless in a way a million massages couldn't achieve.

Brick lifts me carefully and carries me to a new lounger. He disappears and returns with a warm cloth to clean my dripping pussy. "Now you see why I reserved the whole place?"

Oh God. I'm in way over my head. I'm too spent to do anything but nod.

My spa day ends with Brick bundling me up and guiding me to his helicopter. John Acker's in the pilot seat, and I wave, wondering whether he's curious why Brick flew all the way out here himself to pick me up. He's probably paid enough not to be curious.

Still it sits a little weird with me.

Brick and I fly back in silence. He spends the whole time on his phone while I gaze out the window at the setting sun. When we reach the landing pad and the limo, I expect him to go a separate way. But he slides into the backseat beside me.

The fading light gilds his handsome face. There was a strangely bright sheen to his eyes at Miravelle, but now it's gone.

His attention is on his phone again, but I can tell he knows I'm watching him.

"What is it, Madison?" he finally growls.

"Nothing." I force myself to look away. "Today was... lovely," I tell him. "Thank you."

He doesn't reply. He's going to pretend that this was all

within the normal bounds of what a boss would do for his assistant. And that's okay. I need him to pretend, so I can too.

The next thing I know, he's murmuring my name and brushing the hair off my face. I blink my eyes open. In the warm darkness of the backseat, I fell asleep. On his shoulder.

"What–" I jerk back, clearing my throat and gathering myself.

"We're here." The limo's at the curb right in front of Aubrey's and my apartment.

There's a touch of softness in Brick's deep rumble. "Do you need me to help you?"

"No." I swipe a hand across my face. Did I drool on him? I hope not. "I've got it." Tony opens my door, and I scramble out, disoriented by my lack of work clothes. Under my coat, I'm still wearing the soft lounge set Miravelle gave me. That Brick paid for, as a token of appreciation about my work. A typical gift from boss to employee. Nothing unusual here.

"Thanks again," I call and rush to my door. I feel him watching me the whole time.

Nope, nothing unusual here at all.

Tomorrow we'll go back to work and pretend this never happened. That's the only answer to this dilemma. Things are getting too close. It's too much for me to guard my heart against.

Chapter Six

Madi

Madi
I sip my vanilla latte as I shoot off an email congratulating the HR department on their plans for the Christmas party on behalf of my boss, who actually doesn't give a crap.

The elevator dings, and I frown, not expecting to see Blackthroat here today. His beard is looking fuller, and his normally slicked back bangs are a little shaggy, like he's overdue for a haircut. My pussy tingles at the sight.

"This morning is your shareholder's meeting at Adalwulf Associates, sir," I say when he steps off with Eagle. I expected him to go straight to the meeting with his rivals.

"I know. You're coming with us."

"I am?" I shoot to my feet because if that's the case, we must be running late.

"She is?" Eagle repeats.

I grab my coat from the hook and pull it on as I scan the desk. "What do I need? Laptop? Paperwork?"

"Just that smart brain of yours. Maybe a notebook. Listen and remember. That's all. Let's go."

Eagle shoots Blackthroat a look and opens his mouth but then closes it again as if he reconsidered.

I try to quiet the flutters of pleasure in my chest that Blackthroat wants me along. He's come to rely on me. He trusts me.

I don't know why it means so much, but it does. It's impossible for me to untangle whether it's personal or job-related. Especially when I've spent the last two weeks in every possible position on the man's desk.

Which truly gives new meaning to job dedication.

The executive team hates it–Eagle included. I'm not sure how they know we've continued to, ah, *be intimate*, but it's obvious they do.

The three of us step into the elevator. Blackthroat is edgy, with the restless, potent energy he seems to have every morning before we've had sex. He usually demands it first thing, like he can't focus until he gets off. Days like today when his schedule doesn't permit it, he's crabby as hell. Someone usually ends up getting fired or severely dressed down.

Blackthroat draws a deep, audible breath in through his nose and holds it, closing his eyes for a beat.

Funny. I wouldn't have thought of him as a yogic breather. But I'm sure attending this board meeting is a nightmare for him. The Adalwulfs stole the company from him–that has to hurt. It's probably the reason he hates his mom. Was she a part of it?

"What do you know about Adalwulf Associates?" Blackthroat asks.

"It's the hedge fund company owned by members of the Adalwulf family. Officially run by your Uncle, Odin Adalwulf, but his son Aiden is said to oversee the day-to-day business now due to Odin's flagging health. Twelve people sit on the board, including your mother, Catherine Adalwulf, and all her children: you, Ruby, and Scarlett."

Eagle's gaze narrows with what looks like mistrust. "You know quite a bit."

What is he implying? That I've been pumping the boss for personal information while I suck his dick? Does he suspect I'm some kind of corporate spy for the Adalwulfs? I keep my spine straight. "My job requires me to understand the dynamics that affect my boss."

"Does it, though?" Skepticism leaks into Eagle's voice.

"Don't." One word from Blackthroat, and Eagle's expression goes blank. The guard dog heeds his master's command.

My stomach flip-flops. I'm not even sure why. Because Blackthroat protected me? I can't decide if it excites me or makes me nervous. A little of both, I think. I love that I mean something to him, but I also know it won't end well for me. His execs don't like it, and they will look for ways to destroy me.

It's like I can see the jagged teeth of the cliff wall up ahead, the one I'm speeding toward without brakes. Blackthroat isn't safe. He isn't safe for me emotionally, and he may not be safe for my career, either.

If I were smart, I'd call that cosmetics heiress from the charity ball, Eleanor Harrington, the one who offered me a job. It wouldn't hurt to meet with her to have a fall-back plan when things crash and burn here. Because I'm certain now, one way or another, they will crash and burn.

Which is why I put the fifty thousand dollar bonus Blackthroat gave me straight into a savings CD for Brayden's education. Who knows if he can rely on that scholarship when things go south.

"What else do I need to know?" I ask Blackthroat.

He shakes his head. "I don't know. Just pay attention to everything that's said." He's never personable, but this morning he seems grim and distant. Knowing some of his story—or guessing at it—makes my heart ache for him.

"Yes, sir."

The elevator door opens, and we leave the building to get in the back of a limo parked in front. December snow falls in heavy, wet flakes, coating the windows.

Ruby is already seated in the back. Like Brick, her expression is drawn and tight. She's far more tense than when she was stressed at the charity ball. This is different. There's an element of grief to both their countenances, which makes sense. Losing the company must be mingled in with losing their father.

"Hi, Madi," she says softly. "I'm glad you're here."

I work to swallow, trying to unpack what she means by that. She's glad I'm here to support Brick? Like he needs emotional support? Or she's glad I have his back professionally? Or is she personally happy to see me? I can't imagine why that would be the case.

The Adalwulf's second building is just a five minute drive. The limo double-parks in front, and we climb out onto the sidewalk.

Catherine Adalwulf is waiting in the lobby, apparently for us because she nods to the security guard and ushers us to the elevators.

"Why would you wait for us?" Blackthroat demands the moment the elevator doors close.

"Because you're my children," she says simply, ignoring the confrontation in his tone.

"We're not walking in there together like we're united in any way."

"We're united by blood." There's a little more passion in

Catherine's voice now, but I hear angst there, too. Ruby's shoulders hunch, and she doesn't look at her mom or take her side. Eagle puts his hand on her lower back protectively.

"Hi Madi." Catherine catches my eye. She's called the office a couple times since Thanksgiving, making chit chat with me before asking to speak to Brick. Of course, he never takes her calls. It's painful to witness her attempts and his rebuffs. It's obvious they're both hurting over their relationship.

Blackthroat scowls.

I send her a small, polite smile. "Good morning."

What could it be that drove their family apart? It had to be the clients Adawulf poached from the Blackthroat firm. Brick must blame his mother for it.

I'm not the kind of person who takes on the tension of the people around me, so it's like watching an engaging drama unfold. I'm fascinated by it all, recording every nuance and word to mull over later.

We step off the elevator and enter a large conference room with windows on two walls. Most of the seats are already taken by men who all bear a resemblance to Catherine, with sandy blond hair and prominent cheekbones.

The most beautiful one of them all, Aiden Adalwulf, is at the head of the table. He lifts his upper lip in a snarl as we come in. "What's this?" His nostrils flare like I smell bad.

"You've met my assistant." Blackthroat doesn't introduce me by name, not that I expected him to. At least he called me *assistant* instead of *secretary*. I take no offense. Everything about him, from his unnatural good looks to his flat, raspy voice makes my skin crawl. I'd rather not be on his radar.

What does concern me is how Blackthroat's eyes are

still dead. He's gone flat, emotionless–matching Aiden Adalwulf's cold stare. But unlike Aiden, I can feel the emotions raging in Brick. He's not unfeeling, he's holding himself in check. Like barely-contained rage simmers beneath the surface, and he's stepped back emotionally to keep it from erupting.

"She can wait outside," Aiden says.

"No." It's not loud, but there's something in the timber of Blackthroat's voice that makes everyone at the table except for Aiden draw back.

Aiden stands. "This is a confidential meeting."

"She's signed an NDA," Blackthroat says.

"Not for us, she hasn't."

"She stays."

Blackthroat is in a pissing match with his cousin. Even though we're on their turf and Adalwulf's objections are valid, I get the feeling he's going to win. The power behind his demand, his sheer force of will, is enough to shatter glass.

Aiden stares at him for a long beat then sits with a sour look on his narrow face. "Fine. There's nothing to be discussed that won't be made public, anyway."

Ruby rolls her eyes.

There isn't a seat for me at the table, but Blackthroat orders the Adalwulf Associates' assistant, who is pouring water into glasses, to find me one.

She looks to Aiden first and only leaves after he nods. When she returns, she places the chair in the far corner near the door.

Okey dokey. Servants are relegated to corners. I already know this routine from Moon Co. I sit and pull out the notebook and pen, studying everyone at the table.

Nobody else has greeted Brick or Ruby or Eagle. It's

clear the animosity between the two families is thicker than any blood they share.

Aiden calls the meeting to order. As far as I can tell, it's an ordinary board meeting. Minutes are read and approved. Finances reviewed. Ruby and Brick abstain from all votes. In fact, they do nothing but sit and glare at the other board members.

For the life of me, I can't figure out why I'm here, but I stay sharp and take everything in.

The meeting is over in a couple hours, and we all stand to leave. I wait for Blackthroat before heading to the door.

One of the older men drops a sheaf of papers on the floor as he's walking out the door. Aiden jerks back, ramming into me.

In a flash, Blackthroat inserts himself between me and Aiden. *"Don't touch her."* His growl sounds ten times deeper than his normal voice.

Everyone in the room freezes, turning to take in the spectacle.

Jesus.

"It was an accident," I say quickly, trying to de-escalate things.

What on Earth is wrong with Blackthroat? Did he really think his cousin did it on purpose? He looks two seconds away from going for Aiden's throat. His eyes have a strange glow to them.

There's also something strange about Adalwulf's expression. He stares at Blackthroat with what can only be characterized as evil glee.

"I see," he murmurs. *"Interesting."*

Slowly, deliberately, Blackthroat puts his back to Aiden and steers me past him and out the door.

When we get to the elevator, Blackthroat blocks his

mother from getting on, only stepping aside for Eagle and Ruby.

As soon as the elevator doors close, Eagle mutters, "For fuck's sake, Brick." Ruby touches her husband's arm, as if to warn him to stop, but he goes on. "Why did you bring her?"

Blackthroat scrubs a hand across his face. "I don't know."

"You just gave Aiden power, and I don't doubt he's out for blood with you closing Benson despite everything he did to block it."

Ruby nods her agreement, but Blackthroat isn't looking at her, or any of us. He's staring into the distance with a haunted expression.

Eagle goes on, "This is–"

"Stop talking." Brick's words are quiet, but his authority is absolute.

Eagle immediately halts, closing his mouth with a sour expression. Ruby shakes her head, as if in exasperation, but neither of them say another word.

I stare at all three of them, trying to figure out what in the hell is going on, but it's one of the few times in my life that I just can't seem to follow the thread of logic or deduce a pattern from the known facts.

Brick

No one says a word the entire way back to Moon Co. Even Madi, who usually ignores my dictates if she decides they're illogical, stands quietly beside me on the elevator ride up to our floor.

Dammit.

I lost control. I showed Aiden my wolf.

What a colossal fuckup. I honestly don't know why I felt it important to bring Madison to the board meeting, but I did. Shifters rely on their instincts, and mine told me to bring her.

But now Aiden thinks he knows something.

My eyes must have changed color when I faced him. My wolf thought Madison was in danger and went nuts to protect her.

This situation with her is getting out of hand. I've been pretending it's under control. Or that there isn't actually a situation, but after this morning's fiasco, I can't deny it.

Somehow, it feels like another rending of my soul in two directions. Growing up, my love and loyalties were divided. We belonged to our father. We bore his name, were members of his pack. We loved him, and he loved us, but he demanded our absolute loyalty. Drilled into us the weight of the mantle we must wear as his heirs. Me, as his only son and the future alpha of the pack, especially.

But once a week, our mother was allowed to visit. We adored her–she was beautiful, loving, kind. Soft and sweet. She brought us gifts and made us laugh. That one day a week, she showered us with love and attention, except for the hour or so when my father took her upstairs and claimed her.

They hated each other, but the sex kept my father alive. It was part of the bargain struck between the two packs when it became apparent they were fated mates. He kept the young she bore. They kept her.

It's not the same with Madi–she doesn't belong to an enemy pack, but she also doesn't belong to our world. I want her, same as I wanted my mother full-time, but I can't claim her. I need to mate an alpha she-wolf to secure the throne. Then again, who can predict how these things will work?

It's not like a royal bloodline where the son automatically inherits. It's whichever wolf is the most alpha of the pack. Normally, he comes from the same bloodline as the previous alpha, but it doesn't have to be a son. It could be a nephew. Auggie is a strong and smart wolf. He might end up being alpha regardless of who I mate. Or Scarlett might bear the future alpha of the Blackthroat pack when she finds her fated mate.

All I know is that every day that goes by without claiming Madi, I go a little more mad.

I glance over at my lovely assistant. This is the first time I've even allowed my thinking to go this far. The first time I've truly examined the possibilities and ramifications of claiming her. It still seems impossible.

We step off the elevator, and I allow her to precede me. "In my office, please," I murmur.

She darts a glance over her shoulder but obeys, walking ahead and waiting for me to unlock the door and remove my coat and suit jacket.

She shrugs off her coat, hangs it beside mine and waits. Somehow she knows to match me where I am. She's not businesslike or flirty. She's not her usual efficient self, zipping in to take care of my needs. She's simply available.

Because she's our mate, my wolf whispers. *She knows what you need, even when you don't.*

I walk to my desk. My wolf is right, I don't even know what I need now. It's not the hot, aggressive fuck I've been demanding from Madison nearly every morning since Thanksgiving.

I just need *her.* I require her scent to calm me and soothe the rage I have on lockdown beneath my breast-bone. I half-sit on my desk and reach for her, spinning her, so her back comes to my chest, my hand cradling the side of her face. I pull her hair to my nose and inhale deeply.

For a long moment, I don't move. I just let her scent fill my nostrils, trying to find my way back to the alpha I'm supposed to be. The one who didn't get screwed out of a large part of his fortune by his own mother. Who didn't lose his father before he was ready to wear the crown.

The alpha who knows what to do next. About Madison. About the Adalwulfs. About my mother.

"Are we cuddling?" Madison does her usual deflection anytime things get too intimate.

I cover her mouth with my hand, so she can't speak again. She doesn't fight it. She loves the dominance. I know because the scent of her arousal hits my nostrils like a heady aphrodisiac.

I slide my hand down her belly, pulling up the skirt of her dress to get inside her panties. Keeping one hand firmly clamped over her mouth, I take my time exploring her soft folds. Her sweet honey soaks my fingers, and I spread it up through her pleats, coating her clit and making her hips writhe to meet my touch.

I curl two fingers inside her. The angle makes it impossible to get them deep, but I grind the heel of my palm over her clit as I fuck her. She moans and whimpers, licking the hand over her mouth, biting it, taking my thumb into her mouth and sucking it like she's giving me a blowjob. I bring her easily to climax, but still don't have that aggressive urge to bend her over and pound into her, the way I usually do.

But my wolf is right—she knows what I need.

When I release her, she turns and wraps her arms around my neck, reaching up on her tiptoes to kiss my jaw, my neck. She's usually the passive one. I'm the one who takes. Directs. Decides. But she's the aggressor this time.

She unbuttons my trousers as she propels me backward to sit in my chair. My dick is already hard from getting her off, so she frees it from the confines of my briefs and fists the base, pulling hard.

I lean back to enjoy, fascinated by our role reversal. By Madi working to please me. She kneels and takes me into her mouth, swirling her tongue along the underside, teasing the cleft where head meets shaft.

My breath rasps in. Some of the heaviness around me moves. It doesn't dispel, but it shifts around. I register pleasure along with the emotional shitstorm.

Madison works my cock in her mouth for a few minutes, getting me harder than stone, then she rises up, shimmies out of her panties and straddles my waist. "Is this okay?"

"Uh, no, Windows. It's horrible," I say drily. I fist my cock to hold it steady for her as she rises up and lowers her hips down over it. "I hate having my cock sucked and then ridden by my beautiful assistant."

I slide my hands under her skirt and grip her bare ass with both hands, pulling her down and forward to take me fully. She's wetter than a slip 'n slide, gliding over me with mad purpose. She grinds her clit down on the base of my cock as I direct the movement, pulling her forward and back.

I watch her lovely face contort with pleasure, but even as her mouth opens and her nostrils flare, she's studying me right back. I know what she must see—the darkness in me. The shadows and ghosts and pain. I still feel removed from it all. Going to that meeting meant putting my rage under lock and key, so I withdrew.

This brings me back. Being inside her. Having her scent wrap around me. Being near her. This must be the reason I asked her to come along today. On some level, I knew she was the only one who could keep me sane.

Remind me what's important.

But the cost was way too high. Aiden knowing she's my mate? It's disastrous.

I push those thoughts away and surrender to the moment. Changing the direction and rhythm, I lift and lower Madison over me, making her tits bounce in the glorious window I love to hate.

I let out a groan. The sound excites her. She steadies herself with one hand on my shoulder and uses the other to squeeze her own breast. I watch in total fascination. It's enough. Enough distraction from my thoughts to pull me into the moment.

"Come for me, Madi," I murmur.

I used her preferred name again. It slips out in my moments of weakness, but it doesn't matter. I don't need to hold anything over her right now. There's no power struggle today. I'm just a broken man with a wolf on the brink of madness.

She nods. "Yeah." She's breathless, tits bouncing in my face, her soft thighs galloping over my lap.

I grip her ass harder and propel her up and down with more momentum until I find my peak. "Now, Windows."

She comes on command, like the bratty but still obedient little assistant she is.

I groan as I come inside her, and she squeezes and milks my cock. We stay glued together, our breath mingling until it slows.

"Thanks," I say softly as I lift her off and pat her hip, handing her a couple tissues.

As she puts herself together, I catch her watching me,

still attentive to my needs. "Do you need anything? What can I do?"

I shake my head. "You can go."

"I'm canceling your appointments this afternoon."

"No. You don't have to." I'm an alpha wolf. I don't shirk my responsibilities.

"I'm clearing the schedule. My job is to have your back, and you need time alone this afternoon."

A sense of relief washes over me at having her voice the obvious truth. Time alone is definitely what I need.

She stands at the door, fingers wrapped around the door handle without opening it. Despite her determined declaration, she's waiting for my agreement.

"Thank you, Madi."

She shoots me another surprised glance, her expression softening. Something that resembles longing bleeds through before she turns away to hide it.

When she shuts the door, I lean my head back against the chair and groan.

Fuck.

Something needs to be done about Madison. I can't go on like this much longer. Especially now that Aiden knows.

He could turn my pack against me by the weekend, if I don't take command of the situation and act like a fucking alpha.

I'm just not sure I can do what it would take to be that leader.

To get rid of Madi.

Mate a suitable alpha she-wolf.

Prove I'm worthy of my father's legacy.

I'm not sure I even want to keep the pack if it means letting go of the female I'm starting to love.

* * *

Madi

I leave Blackthroat's office on trembling legs.

Whatever I thought of the man, it all changed today. He's so much more than the hardened, heartless asshole I once believed him to be, and today I glimpsed what made him that way. The grief and destruction he's faced. The ghosts that haunt him.

No man without a heart would suffer as deeply as I saw him suffer today. And despite my reluctance to get close to the man, this did it.

There's nothing I wouldn't do to take that pain from him if I could.

I cancel all his calls and clear his schedule for the rest of the day. It's a small gesture, but it's one thing I can do to lighten the load from his shoulders.

I also decide to send an email to Eleanor Harrington. Not because I want to leave Moon Co–just to have options. I'm a practical person who likes to have backup plans. Following up with a friendly email won't hurt anything.

When I'm finished, I check in with the HR department about the Christmas party Friday night to make sure they have everything under control. We've rented a banquet hall at The Four Seasons and booked a live band. It will be a formal event with an open bar, lots of prizes, games, and celebrations. We wanted it to be something employees look forward to every year, not an awkward event they have to suffer through.

My phone rings with a number I immediately recognize. I pick up.

"Hi sweetheart, it's Catherine Adalwulf. Do you have a few minutes to chat?"

I glance toward Brick's shut door. "Actually, yes. This is a good time for me."

"Is Brick there?"

I don't answer her question because it would be inappropriate for me to share any personal information related to my boss with anyone who calls, even his mother. "What can I do for you?" I ask politely instead.

"Madi, I'll be frank with you. You saw today how awful things are between my side of the family and my children."

"Yes."

"Brick blames me for the takeover, and I've never had a chance to explain what really happened. He won't take my calls. He won't meet with me. He wouldn't speak to me at Thanksgiving. I've tried writing letters, but they go unanswered. I have to assume he doesn't read them. I'm just wondering...sweetheart, I want to make things right with him. I want to have a chance to heal this wound between us, so we can hopefully find forgiveness and form some kind of relationship together going forward. I'm not out to hurt him. I hope you believe that."

I make a non-committal sound. I'm the type who reserves judgment, but I do tend to believe her. Of course, it's not my place to take sides or judge anyone for anything that happened in their past. This is none of my business. I'm just the assistant. Or so I keep trying to believe.

"I'm not asking you to advocate for me or take my side in any way. I just want to get Brick alone for fifteen or twenty minutes. I haven't been able to do that in all the years since his father died."

"I see." Now I know exactly where this is going.

"Madi, is there any way you could arrange something? I know you're in charge of his schedule. He wouldn't agree to meet with me, but could you set up an appointment he won't question? He will refuse it if he knows it's me, so it would have to be under the radar."

Tension tugs in my solar plexus. I do want to help her, actually. Well, no, I want to help Blackthroat, and in this case, that might mean going against his wishes. She's right about the situation needing to be healed. My boss is in pain, and if a meeting with his mom could help stop his suffering, then I should help make it happen. My job is to make his life easier. Wouldn't it be easier if he healed his relationship with his mother?

Ugh. I'm not sure. This is a slippery slope.

I click open Blackthroat's electronic calendar and scan through his appointments for the week.

"He's out of the office for an appointment Monday. You could come here and wait in his office to talk to him when he gets back."

"Oh, honey, that would be great." Relief and appreciation sound in her voice.

"Okay, be here around one o'clock."

"I will. Thank you Madi."

I hang up and a coil of anxiety twists behind my belly button.

I hope I didn't just make a huge mistake.

Chapter Seven

Billy
      I drive to Williamsburg, the Brooklyn neighborhood where Madison Evans lives, and find valet parking in a hotel nearby. The private investigators I hired gave me the full scoop on her, including a dossier on her roommate, Aubrey Cook. The two apparently grew up in the same apartment building in Jersey.

It's Aubrey I'm hunting down today. There's not a logical reason—nothing I think I can glean from her that my private investigators probably couldn't ferret out. But my instincts told me to visit her in person, and a wolf trusts his instincts.

I stare at the photo of a beautiful young woman with dark skin and a froth of wild brown curls highlighted in gold and crimson. Her skin is smooth, her cheekbones high, and her pierced nose is adorned with a thin gold hoop. She's pleasing to the eye, but I hate everything about her. I can just tell she's a screaming liberal. She has a wild and carefree look that puts my teeth on edge. The photo was taken from her social media, and in it, she's wearing a pair of cut-off jean shorts and a crop top that reads, "Eat the Rich." As if by rejecting money, she might actually hold some kind of power, when of course, the opposite is always true.

I leave the folder with her information in the car, along with my necktie, and walk to La Résistance, the cafe where she'll be working this evening.

Why a cafe would be open at night is beyond me. Shouldn't coffee places close after dark? It speaks of a business that doesn't really know who or what it is. My opinion is confirmed when I arrive at the establishment. The wall outside is painted with a giant mural depicting an Occupy Wall Street protest. Inside, I find an arty, activist sort of place with a bulletin board covered in flyers advertising everything from social protest events to art openings and open mics.

I see my prey behind the counter. Her hair is in braids now that cascade over her shoulders and swing and shift with each movement. She wears a tight, cinnamon-colored crop top with a heart cut-out above her breasts in the style her roommate Madi likes to wear to torment Brick. The curves of her ass are clearly delineated in a tight pair of jeans.

I gnash my teeth, already wanting to wring her smug little neck for being as big a cocktease as her friend.

Unlike Madison, Aubrey doesn't play act at fitting within a business world where she doesn't belong. She seems very clearly at home in this wild, chaotic environment of the cafe.

According to her file, she's majoring in Women's Studies on the five or six-year plan because she's putting herself through school with loans and her job here. My PI believes she may be angling for pre-law eventually based on her extracurricular activities and social activism, but it's hard to tell.

The mere fact that this person is Madison Evans' best friend speaks volumes. I'd suspected Madison was faking who she was, and this seems to confirm it.

She watches me survey the place, unwrapping a blow pop and sticking it in her mouth as I saunter forward.

Unlike Madi, she makes no polite pretense at being helpful. She doesn't snap to attention when I walk to the counter. She doesn't even take the damn blow pop from between those pillowed lips, just leans on her forearms, giving me an admittedly glorious view of her cleavage.

"Are you lost?" Her voice is whiskey on the rocks. Startlingly smooth.

But an even bigger surprise is her scent. It hits me, nearly knocking me backward. It has earthy tones, honey and nutmeg with hints of Egyptian spices. I fight the hold it has on me because it comes on like a full assault. Energy surges within my cells–sending forth a burst of power. It feels like the ferocity of a hunt combined with the release of four orgasms packed into one.

For a moment, I can't think. All I can do is blink, continuing to drag in that dangerous aroma. To solve my dilemma, I stop breathing. I hold my inhale until my head clears, and then I let it slowly out.

"Why do you ask that?"

She sweeps her gaze up and down my body, and I realize what she sees. Even without the tie, I'm far too well-dressed for this place in my two thousand dollar Armani suit and nine hundred dollar shoes. I shake my cuff down over my Rolex.

She takes a long suck on the blow pop, and my dick

jerks in my trousers, apparently jealous. She removes it with a popping sound. "You look lost."

"I'll take an espresso."

She lifts up off her forearms but doesn't scurry to make my drink. Like she thinks I have all the time in the world to stare at her staring at me. She gives a slow nod. "You look like an espresso man."

My upper lip curls. "What does that mean?"

She lifts an elegant shoulder, turning away like she has better things to do. I can't tell whether she's making my drink or not. She moves around behind the counter, still in no apparent rush.

I try to control my rage—at least that's what I think it is, except it's so tinged with sexual tension, it almost renders me helpless.

It's absurd to let a human's scent affect me. She's attractive, sure. But the farthest thing from my type. So far, I wouldn't even fuck her as a one-off.

I'm not sure my dick agrees, though, so I drag my gaze away from her ass to scan the bulletin board behind the counter. This one isn't covered in flyers, it's packed with photos.

Lots of them feature the lovely barista Aubrey. Apparently, she's been working here for years because in some of them, she appears young—still a teen.

And then my gaze snags on something interesting.

My wolf snarls with satisfaction. This is why my instincts told me to come here. Not because the human has a scent that makes me forget every woman I've ever had writhing beneath me. Not because she makes me want to break my hard rule of never, ever dallying with a human.

No. It's exactly what I came here seeking.

A photo of Aubrey and Madison and an older woman with a shaved head holding Occupy Wall Street signs.

I knew she was a fraud!

I knew there was something off about Madison the moment I met her, and this proves it. Why would she take a job on Wall Street if she hates it? Supposedly to help pay her brother's college tuition, but he got a scholarship, and she's still at Moon Co, doing her best to wrap my alpha around her pinkie finger.

I know who she's really working for. Her first month at Moon Co, Madison came into the office smelling like the Adalwulfs. She claimed she went into their building accidentally, but I don't believe it.

And then there was the way Aiden Adal-fuck showed interest in her. He pretended to want to order her from the room, but it was a test to see what Brick would do. He knows the human is Brick's weakness.

Worse are the rumors the Adalwulfs are circulating. I have spies embedded in their pack, and they report the seeress has a new prophecy. *The Blackthroat king has a weakness. She will destroy all he desires.*

It might be bogus. The crone has been right before, but it would be Machiavellian, to plant a human near Brick to tempt him and then spread a fake rumor of a prophecy.

Whether or not the prophecy is true doesn't matter. If the Blackthroat pack hears about the prophecy and learns about Brick's obsession with his secretary, they'll put two and two together. They'll fear for their Alpha. The stronger will question his ability to lead us. The weaker might defect. Energized by a crack in our foundation, the Adalwulfs will rally to destroy us.

And if the prophecy is true...it could mean the beginning of the end. I have to stop it.

Madison Evans is part of a plot to bring Brick down. I know it. I just need proof.

Behind me, someone drops a dish and breaks it. "Sorry," the guy yells as Aubrey's head whips around. He stoops to pick up the pieces.

"Don't worry about it. I'll get it." She finishes brewing my espresso and hands me the tiny, steaming cup, then abandons her post behind the counter to disappear in the back.

I down the shot of coffee, then walk around the counter, pretending to look for a napkin in case anyone sees me, and grab the photo off the board.

I pocket it as I walk out of the cafe.

Madison Evans, the jig is up. I'm onto you, and as soon as I figure out exactly what your game is and when the Adalwulfs hired you to play it, you're going down.

Chapter Eight

Brick

Monday, I walk out of the elevator after getting my hair cut, and I catch a scent of a female that instantly puts me on edge.

My mother.

Like everything about her, it inspires conflict within me. The scent activates all the pleasure of my childhood memories. Of the female who loved me. Doted on me. Was my entire world one day a week.

I've had to deregulate that response to remind myself she's a traitor. She killed my father and can't be forgiven or trusted again.

Ever.

I look around but don't see her. Did she just visit, or is she still here? Dammit, I knew she was going to use Madison to get to me.

"Where is she?" I snarl at Madison, who keeps her composure, as always.

"In the conference room."

"Get rid of her."

Madison hesitates, sliding a hand up the back of her neck like she's considering.

Dammit. I don't know what there is to consider. I give an order, and I expect it to be obeyed. I'm completely out of temper, as I always am when it comes to my mother.

Rather than deal with Madison's insubordination, I march to the conference room to take care of the situation myself. I stand in the doorway. My mother is already on her feet, wringing her hands.

"*Out.*" I make it easy for both of us and use the alpha command in my voice.

Her feet move her toward the door even as her mouth starts up. "Brick I want to tell you about the night your father died. I didn't know—"

"*Silence.*"

Again, alpha's command renders her speechless. I step back to let her pass, but as soon as she's out the door, that spontaneous impulse to obey me wears off, and she reaches for my arm.

"Brick, please can we just hash this out?"

"*Out of the building.*" This time I make sure I use enough force in the wavelength of my voice to make it last.

She stumbles toward the elevators.

Dammit, if I don't reach for her elbow to steady her. She's still my mother.

The knife she stabbed me with the night she killed my father twists in my chest, delivering fresh pain. Especially when I catch the scent of her tears.

Trapped in her blue gaze, I find myself offering the only explanation I have. "I can't."

A tear tracks down her face, and she nods, squeezing my hand at her elbow before walking away.

I don't move until she's in the elevator, and it's moving down, and then I round on Madison.

"Who do you work for?" I demand.

She stands for the dressing down, appropriately deferential, which does nothing to stop my tirade. "You, sir."

I nod. "Do you make appointments for me you know I don't want to take?"

"No, sir."

Confounded at how she could do this to me, I drop the boss-assistant thing. "You *know* how I feel about her. Why would you blindside me like that?"

Madison pulls in a sharp breath, and a tear streaks down her face.

Fuck. It's even worse than seeing my mom cry. Way worse. All the anger and aggression drops from my body.

And now I know for certain what she is to me. My mate. The scent of a mate's tears has the ability to instantly lower a male's testosterone levels. It's nature's safety mechanism to prevent violence in a shifter's home. Alpha wolves are aggressive, jealous and protective, but one whiff of their mate's tears, and they're brought to their knees.

I shove my hands in my pockets, the need to soothe her becomes more important than anything else.

Now that I can think, I try to decode her actions. Madison has never acted against me before. She's loyal, and she protects me and my time. What would make her screw me like this?

"Did she force you?"

Madi shakes her head.

I study her. Her posture is stiffened, prepared for my rebuke, but her expression is resolute. No, Madison thinks through every action she takes. She did this on purpose, knowing I would be this angry which means... I arrive at the answer. "You thought this was the best for me."

She nods, sniffing.

I close my eyes in exasperation then open them again. "Madi, you had no right. You don't know what she did."

"You're right." She blinks rapidly to clear her eyes. "All I know is that you're hurting as a result of your relationship with her, and she's trying very hard to fix it." Another tear streaks down her face. "I'm sorry. I shouldn't have let her in here. I won't do it again."

I cup the back of her head. Her tears are killing me. "Please don't cry."

"Am I fired?"

My chest constricts. The very idea of her not being in this office with me makes my wolf want to tear the building down. I force lightness into my voice. "You're unfireable, remember?"

She gives a watery laugh.

"I'm sorry I yelled at you."

"No, you don't owe me an apology. I deserved it."

"No one deserves my temper, especially not you." I kiss her temple and thumb away the moisture under her eye. Tipping my head toward my office, I offer a small smile. "Make it up to me?"

I sense her relief that I turned it back to sex–the only place where we're fully honest and unguarded with each other. She pushes off her desk, and I take her hand to lead her inside. I lock the door, and when I turn, she reaches for my belt, unlooping it from the buckle.

I watch, fascinated, as always, when she takes charge. I like when she gives to me. There are very few people in my life I trust enough to show up for me, and she's quickly becoming one of them.

She unbuttons my pants and lowers to her knees. I groan when she releases my shaft and takes it into her mouth.

"You're beautiful," I murmur as she works her mouth up and down, sucking hard on the outstrokes, using her fist to trail behind her mouth, so it feels like my entire dick is engulfed, not just half.

She lifts her gaze to mine, holding it. Showing me she's paying attention, that she'll deliver everything I need, as she always does.

I brush the backs of my fingers across her cheek, stroke her hair back from her face and hold it taut behind her head.

She's so lovely. So perfect. What am I going to do about her?

I can't cut her loose, and I can't have her. Every day, it's killing me a little more. I'm keeping moon madness at bay with the sex, but I'm rapidly reaching the point when that won't be enough. I'll have to mark her or die.

"Madison," I murmur on a sigh.

She sucks harder, moves her head faster. As the pleasure starts to wash over me, I tighten my grip in her hair and hold her head still, arcing in and out of her mouth.

"That's it, beautiful. Take me deep. Relax that throat." I slow down, so she can follow my orders, and she does, allowing me to push deeper. Heat sweeps over me. My balls tighten and lift.

"Are you going to swallow for me, Madi?"

She gives a muffled assent around my cock, and I let her take over the action. She grips my ass with one hand, uses her fist with the other and bobs over my cock like she's competing in the blow job Olympics.

I let out a growl that sounds more wolf than man, but I

can't stop myself. I bark and then come down her throat. She swallows and swallows and then sucks me clean.

"Good girl. So fucking good." I caress her cheek and help her to her feet before I tuck my dick away.

"Are you okay?" She looks a little dazed, but I'm not asking about the post-sex state, I'm asking about our fight. I know I can be a real bastard when I'm bent out of shape, and the last time I took it out on her, I nearly lost her.

"I'm sorry I made you cry. Did I scare you?"

She shakes her head.

"No, you're not scared of me. You were torn over your decision."

"Yes." She looks sorry, and I want to punch my own face for being a dick to her. She cares about me–enough to try to fix the holes in my life.

I stroke her face. "You're a special person, Madison. One of a kind."

She falls into me, and I wrap my arms around her. Hugging is not normally part of our repertoire–it's usually some form of rough sex, often with a flavor of degradation or power exchange because that's what turns her on.

This is more intimate than anything we've done up to now.

"My mom murdered my dad."

I surprise myself with the words. I had no plan of telling her–ever. Yet now I've said them, and I can't take them back.

She gasps, horrified, and pulls away to stare up at me.

It's too intense. I look past her, out the wall-to-wall windows in my office.

"A-re you sure?"

I nod.

"Did she get arrested? Could they prove it? I never read anything about it in my–"

"We didn't report it," I cut in. Wolves don't involve human law enforcement in pack matters.

"Brick, you should have."

I love when she uses my first name. My wolf finds it satisfying on some shallow level.

"She's my mother, Madi. What was I going to do? Put her in prison?"

Madi claps a hand over her mouth, her expressive brown eyes welling with tears. "My God–I'm so sorry. I can't *imagine*."

"So you can see why I don't like her showing up at Thanksgiving or at the office."

A tear slips from her eye.

"Don't." I thumb it away. "It kills me when you cry. Please don't."

She sniffs and shakes her head. "I won't."

Now I want to kick myself. It's not fair to ask her to hold it in or fight it. But her logical brain comes online. "H-how did she do it?"

"Poison." Silver dust mixed in with the tobacco. Silver is poisonous to shifters. Totally debilitating. "She brought my dad a gift. She'd gone to Cuba and brought him cigars–his favorite. They were poisoned. When he smoked the first one, it went straight into his lungs and killed him immediately."

Her eyes swim with tears, but she blinks them back. "That's horrible. Are you sure it was her? I mean, she brought the cigars, but did she know about the poison? Were they out of her or your father's control any time between her giving them to him and him smoking them?"

I leave Madison and walk to the windows to look out at

the city below. Her questions are valid, but I resent every one of them. I don't want to open this can of worms–I've never wanted to. It was hard enough to assimilate what happened without examining it all too closely.

"If it wasn't her, it was her family. My uncle or even my great-grandmother, who is a seriously creepy old woman. It doesn't matter. My mom was the instrument of his death."

Madison walks up behind me. In the glass, I see her reach out, then pull her hand back, like she's afraid I won't receive her touch. "Is it the same, though? Her knowing and participating versus being the unwitting instrument? Those are pretty different things, aren't they?"

"To me, it's the same." My voice sounds dead.

The Adalwulfs killed my father and stole his company. My mother is an Adalwulf. These things can't be separated. I can't forgive her, no matter what her part in it was.

"You see her as complicit, whether she acted directly or not," Madison guesses.

"Exactly."

"What if she wasn't?"

I whirl on her, and she immediately throws her hands up in surrender. "I'm not trying to piss you off. I just think it's important to have all the facts before making judgments. Especially about things that are close to the heart. Like your own mother." She adds the last part softly, and I tug her against my body and kiss the top of her head.

Her scent smooths my frayed temper.

"Your input has been noted," I murmur against her silky hair. "Call my pilot and have him bring the helicopter around. I need to get some fresh air."

She lifts her head, brow furrowed. "You're going to the Berkshires?"

"Yes. You can leave for the day," I say, even though it's only three in the afternoon.

"I can't. I need to finish up those reports. My boss is a real dick." She tilts her head when I don't respond. "That was a joke, of course."

"Finish them in the morning."

"I'd rather finish them tonight. Are you trying to get rid of me?"

"No." I shrug although it does feel wrong to leave her working here after I've put her through the wringer today. But this is why I value her as an assistant. Even without her scent. That hot as fuck body. Even without the attraction, she'd still be the best employee I've ever had.

* * *

Madi

I stay late working. I'm a perfectionist by nature, but I'm sure some of my workaholism tonight is guilt-driven. I screwed up with Brick today, and I hate screwing up. My heart aches for him. I can't imagine the level of pain he must feel to believe his mother actually killed his father.

I believe there are layers of the trauma that need to be peeled back. I'm not as apt to blindly believe his mother was responsible based on circumstantial evidence, but it's obvious he's not willing to unpack it. It's all too sore for him.

I check my cell phone to see if Aubrey responded to my text, and I see an email has come into my personal account from Eleanor Harrington at Torrent Cosmetics. A shard of guilt stabs at me, but I push it back. I've done nothing disloyal to Brick by contacting her. It's not like I'm going to leave this job. I just want to have a back-up plan in place for when things crumble because I feel certain they will.

Her email is brief but warm.

Madison,

Sorry for my delayed response—I just got back from Paris. I was hoping I would hear from you. I would love to get together. I have lunch free on Friday. Meet me at Tiffany's at noon?

Eleanor

Huh. She signed it "Eleanor." Somehow, I wouldn't have pegged her as a friendly first-name-only type. She seemed crustier than that. I also never dreamed she'd suggest a lunch rather than a phone call or an interview at her office. It seems almost like a social call rather than business. But that doesn't make sense.

Friday is not ideal as it's the company holiday party, and I need to be around to field the demands on Blackthroat, but I also don't want to miss this opportunity. I respond that I will be there and put it on my calendar, so he'll know I'm going to be away. Hopefully it won't blow up in my face.

Jerry, the janitor, is already almost finished with cleaning our floor when I finally get ready to leave.

"The boss is already gone, huh?" He sends me a friendly smile. He's used to seeing us both in here late.

"Yep. He left early for a change."

"So why are you still here?"

I shrug. "Trying to get ahead of him, I guess." It's just small talk.

Jerry's an older guy in his sixties but still totally fit. He wears jeans and flannel shirts, which always strikes me as odd because the rest of the janitors I've seen around the building wear blue Dickies uniforms.

"Jerry, I love that you get to wear jeans to work. How is it you have special privileges?"

"Aw, I work after hours, so no one has to see what I wear." He waves a gloved hand at me. "No one except you and the big boss when you're here burning the midnight oil."

Big Bad Boss.

My chest tightens again thinking of Blackthroat. It's striking how different I feel about him now that he's shown me his vulnerabilities.

"But even when I leave, the janitorial staff on the first level is in uniform."

"Ah, they said you were bright. You know what, Madi? I just wear whatever I damn well please. I'm supposed to wear those costumes, but I don't like the way they feel."

My brain stutters on the *they said you were bright*.

Who said that? Why would the janitor be discussing me with anyone? Particularly anyone who knows me?

"You see, my family goes way back with the Black-throats. We've always worked for them. So Moon Co doesn't fuss much with me. Did you ever wonder why I'm the only one allowed to clean the executive offices? They want it to be someone they trust to prevent corporate espionage and all that."

Huh. I actually hadn't wondered, but it makes sense. I guess it's always who you know on Wall Street. Even for the janitorial positions.

I stand and gather my things. "Are you finishing up? Should I get the lights?"

"No, I'll get them, Madi. You head on home. I've got everything here taken care of."

"Okay, goodnight."

I take the elevator downstairs, sagging against one wall as I immediately forget Jerry and return to the problem of Brick and his mother. What an awful situation.

My energy reserves feel empty, and I realize I haven't eaten much today. I put in an order for eggplant lasagna and ask Tony if he'll drop me off at the restaurant again. A short walk to stretch my legs and a hot meal will do me good.

There's a black limo parked in front of the restaurant when I come out. At first, I think it's Tony, waiting for me even though I told him I needed a walk. But there's a different driver behind the wheel. For one brief, heart-flopping moment, I think it might be Brick, until I remember he left in the helicopter.

I head towards my apartment, cutting between buildings. The wind is icy, and I duck my head.

The limo follows me. I slow my steps as it stops. The driver hops out and opens the back door and beckons toward it, as if I could get in. "Ms. Evans," he says, as if we know each other. Which we don't. He's not Tony or Blackthroat's driver.

I don't know what's going on.

I walk a little closer, eyeing the darkened interior of the limo. I'm not dumb enough to get in a strange car, not even when it's a limo, but I'm curious.

"Madison."

I recognize the creepy, rasping voice, before the fair-haired man in a long, dark coat climbs out of the limo. Aiden Adalwulf.

I back away slowly. I'm in a quiet alleyway between brick buildings. The narrow street is a shortcut, and it's well lit, but typically empty.

Not tonight. Up ahead, a big guy strolls towards me, his sleek suit doing nothing to narrow the bulk of his arms and shoulders. He looks like one of the bodyguards who flanked Aiden when he accosted me at the coffee shop. Behind me, just past the limo, his twin closes in. They're both huge, taking up more than their fair share of the alley, strolling slowly like they don't have a care in the world. I know without a doubt that they're here to stop me from escaping before I talk to their boss.

On a scale of one to swiping right on Patrick Bateman, how much trouble am I in?

Aiden is a respectable businessman. Sure, he's cutthroat, but what Wall Street executive isn't? And yes, he gives off serial killer vibes, but he wouldn't literally cut my throat. At least not here, in the middle of a bustling neighborhood. Shops and restaurants full of people are only a block away.

Aiden wouldn't do it himself. He wouldn't risk blood staining his ten thousand dollar suit.

Better to not flinch. *Rule number one.* The more confident I act, the more power I hold onto.

I face him. "Yes?"

"I'd like to offer you a job."

I stifle my first instinct, which is to scream *No* and run away. I clench my jaw and wait for him to expound.

"Assistant to the CEO," he continues in that evil robot voice. "Double whatever pay and benefits Blackthroat is giving you now."

I raise my brows. "Double?" I echo. I once took a negotiating class, and the teacher drilled two basic skills into us over and over. Either keep silent or repeat the last thing the person on the other side of the table says.

"To start. You obviously have valuable skills and experience. It would take very little training for you to get up to speed. On the Benson deal, for example."

I nod slowly, pretending to think things over. "Thank you for your offer. I'm flattered that you took the time to corner me in a dark alley to give it to me, but I must respectfully decline." There, just enough sarcasm to get the point across. I pivot away and continue walking as fast as I can without spilling my dinner. The beefy bodyguard looms in front of me, blocking my way, but if I'm fast, I can swing my take-out bag, give him a face full of eggplant lasagna, and hope the surprise gives me enough time to slip past.

"Come back, Madison," Aiden calls.

I have no intention of obeying, but something in his voice makes me stop and turn. It's like my body doesn't belong to my own mind.

"How much does he pay you?"

I hate that I'm walking back to him. I don't even know why I'm doing it. "That's none of your business, is it, Mr. Adalwulf?"

His lips twitch, like he finds my rudeness amusing. "I'll double it."

"I'm happy with my current arrangement."

"I'll bet you are." His eyes glitter silver under the streetlights. "How long have you been fucking your boss?"

I've been expecting someone to say it to me, but for some reason it still gets under my skin. I'm usually great with snappy comebacks, but nothing surfaces, so I whirl on my heel to truly leave this time.

"Madison, did he tell you his secret?"

I stop again. Dammit. There's nothing more aggravating than a dangled puzzle to solve. "What secret?"

Aiden saunters toward me, his shined shoes clacking on the broken pavement, his long coat flapping open as he steps. I'm both repulsed and fascinated by the spectacle he makes. Even the shadows don't hide the fact that he's as handsome as Brick. Fair where Brick is dark. Slick and falsely-friendly where Brick is jagged-edged and surly.

"You don't know?" His lips twist into a wicked smile. "Interesting. He doesn't plan on keeping you, then."

My heart thunders in my chest. What does he mean by that? I know this guy is fucking with me, but I can't stand when I don't understand what's going on.

"Nobody's keeping anybody," I snap. "We're human beings with free will."

Aiden snorts. "Oh, sweetheart. You really have no clue." He gives me a mock-sympathetic look, reaching out to touch my cheek with his gloved fingers.

I frown, trembling although I'm not sure what has me so riled up. Goosebumps raise on my arms. "Why are you here?" I demand as I try to piece together the conversation and his possible motives for coming.

He didn't really think he'd lure me away with the promise of a higher wage, so what was his goal?

"Mm. I heard you were smart," he says in a strange echo of what Jerry just said to me. "Not smart enough, though."

The asshole steals my dramatic exit, by turning and striding back to his limo, impossibly graceful for such a large man.

Chapter Nine

Madi

Full confession–I've never even been inside Tiffany's before. The Blue Box Cafe is as much an artistic experience as it is culinary, with a bright but luxurious setting. I have that nineties song "Breakfast at Tiffany's" playing in my head–it's another favorite oldie of Aubrey's–as I walk in.

I have to fight the feeling of not belonging with every step I take. Good thing I'm adept at faking it. Perhaps it's a test–Ms. Harrington wants to know if my table manners are good enough before she brings me into her fold.

I'm ushered to the older woman where she sits in a prime spot by a window. She stands when I approach. I extend my hand and she clasps it with both hands.

Weird.

"Madison. I love that you contacted me."

A waiter appears to push in her chair when she sits back down.

He comes to mine, but I'm already sitting.

"Yes, thank you for seeing me." I open my attaché case

and fish out the crisp resume I printed on a translucent vellum paper. I assume Torrent Cosmetics has a twenty-first century HR department where you upload all pertinent materials, but I'm guessing Ms. Harrington is old-school and likes to hold something in her hand while she interviews.

She takes the resume but doesn't look at it.

"I should start by saying I'm not actively looking for a position at the moment. I just want to keep my options open in case things change where I am."

Eleanor arches a manicured brow. "That's an excellent negotiation tactic. Are you trying to work me, your present employer, or both?"

"Neither at the moment." I'm unruffled by her attempt to call me out. "As I said, it's purely networking."

She nods, apparently liking my answer. "You seem quite bright." She glances at my resume. "You graduated from Princeton with a perfect GPA and landed a position with a notoriously hard-to-work-for CEO."

I incline my head. I'm feeling guiltier by the moment for being here. This was a mistake.

"Moreover, your current boss appeared annoyed when I attempted to poach you."

"I'm flattered you even offered me your card."

"I know potential when I see it." She verbally pats herself on the back. "Tell me about yourself. Things I wouldn't find on this resume." She waves the paper in the air.

I hesitate. What is there to say? That paper contains the whole of what I would show to anyone who isn't extremely close to me.

"At the moment, my work takes up most of my time, so I can't say I have any interesting hobbies, unless you count beating my own record at how fast I can complete a New York Times crossword."

Eleanor laughs, as if I'm particularly amusing. I'm honestly not used to interviewers being this warm and fuzzy.

The waiter stops by, and I order a salad for lunch. I need to keep this meeting short so Blackthroat doesn't get annoyed.

"How do you find working on Wall Street? I wouldn't have expected a sociology major to end up there."

"No, I wasn't planning on it, but the opportunity arose, and it seemed the sort of thing to do while I'm young."

"You didn't consider graduate studies?" She studies me with great curiosity.

It's a strange line of questioning.

"I did, actually. I was accepted at Harvard and Yale" – I'm not above a good name-drop when I'm being inter-viewed by a Manhattan socialite– "but, I decided a change of pace was in order."

"Aren't you just a glorified secretary, now, though?"

I give her a professional, unruffled smile. "A very well-paid one."

She sits back with a smug expression. "So it was about the money."

I don't let my irritation show. "The money and the chal-lenge. You mentioned that my employer is notoriously diffi-cult. I found that challenge appealing."

A knowing smile spreads across Eleanor's face. "And you succeeded in meeting the challenge, as you apparently have succeeded at everything you've tried."

Ms. Harrington's interview style is an interesting mix of jabs and compliments. I suppose she's trying to keep me on my toes.

Our food comes, and I attend to it, trying to keep this lunch from drawing out any longer than it already has.

"What sort of position did you have in mind for me?" I ask, not because I'm actually considering it, but to turn the interview around, so I'm asking the questions.

"Something similar. Assistant to the CEO." She puts her hand on her chest. "*Moi*. I've been looking for a young protege I can mold in my image, and I think you might have the brains and grit to fill the position."

I draw in a breath, somewhat taken aback.

What could I possibly offer that any other Ivy League graduate couldn't? What is it about me that makes her believe I'm moldable to her image?

"Well...that's extremely flattering. As I said, I'm not looking for a new position at present."

"Yes. I imagine it's quite exciting on Wall Street. But at Torrent Cosmetics, you'd be a part of it all–creative challenges, business negotiations, marketing a billion dollar empire. Surely that appeals to your sense of challenge."

My heart beats erratically. The achiever in me is tempted by the position. Especially knowing things with Brick could blow up any day. But that fundamentally loyal part of me refuses to walk away.

Not until things actually do implode.

He's become something integral to my identity and purpose. I need to see this thing out with him, whatever it is.

"Is this a limited-time offer, or would you be open to me contacting you in the future when my situation changes?"

The older woman appears slightly disappointed but not surprised. "Contact me any time, Madison. I'm interested in you. I'd like to see you at Harrington now or in the future."

Color me surprised. It's an unheard-of opportunity. I'm used to working hard for things, not having them dropped in my lap. Apparently my position with Blackthroat has raised my social status more than I realized.

"Thank you so much for your offer–and for lunch." I wipe my mouth, set down my napkin and stand. "I do need to get back to work, but I appreciate your time and consideration."

"Stay in touch, Madison."

I walk out, feeling more confused and guilty than I was walking in. Am I really turning down the opportunity of a lifetime to stay in a situation I know will end up crushing me emotionally if not professionally?

Yes, I am. Because even though I know I'm racing toward a cliff's edge, nothing would stop me so long as Brick Blackthroat is involved.

* * *

Brick

Madison left the building for a lunch appointment. I'm already edgy as hell because she seemed cagey about where she was going, but when she comes into my office smelling like Eleanor Harrington, my wolf rages.

Those damn high society humans. We mix with people like the Harringtons at our charity events. We'll take their money, we'll manage their investments, but they are nothing like us.

I'm not pissed at Madison. Scratch that. I definitely am, but my wolf isn't. My wolf wants to protect her.

Sully believes she is, most likely, the unacknowledged daughter of Brett Harrington, Eleanor's son. It's not clear whether he knows he has a daughter and wants nothing to do with her or whether he's been in the dark the entire time.

What is clear is that Eleanor anonymously paid for

Madison's prep school education and made phone calls that ensured her entry into Princeton with a generous financial aid package. I gauge Madison's mood. She doesn't seem shaken up or disturbed now, not like she would if she'd just learned the old lady's secret.

"I'm sure you remember the company holiday ball is tonight." She's in a sweater dress with cutout shoulders and a peek-a-boob chest. I already had her up against the window this morning, but I'm feeling territorial, and that makes me desperate to get inside her again.

"Yes." I purposely direct my attention at my computer because I'm not fully in control at the moment. My wolf needs to tone it the fuck down.

"I have to be there early, but we need you there by seven or eight to formally greet everyone."

"We'll drive over together," I clip, still not looking her way.

"I have to be there by five-thirty to make sure everything is running smoothly."

Now I give her my full attention, and it's with the air of a reprimand. "When I gave you the task of liaising with HR for the party, it was not for you to run it. It was for you to represent me and my interests. You're not their staff; you're mine. So you'll go when I go."

My wolf is disgruntled by the lie. She's not mine. Not the way he needs her to be.

She hesitates for a beat. "You're the boss."

"Big Bad Boss," I mutter as she turns to sail away.

"Madison." I catch her before she reaches the door, my tone business-like.

She pivots. "Yes, sir?" She still plays subordinate seamlessly which tells me what I always suspected—that it's been an act and a game from the very start. I never had her respect, nor her fear.

Why do I love that so much?

"With whom did you have lunch?"

She hesitates a second before tossing back, "Why do you ask?"

"Answer the question."

She must hear I'm not fooling around, but she still cocks a hip. "Am I not allowed to take a lunch break?"

I don't answer. Don't release her from my gaze. But I should remember that Madison has negotiation skills that far exceed her age or station. She simply lifts a brow, staring right back.

"Are you looking for a new job?" My voice is deadly now because the thought of losing her makes my wolf surge to the surface. He's jealous. Possessive.

Very, very dangerous.

Regret flickers over Madison's face, and my wolf thrashes beneath the surface. "No. Though I am keeping my options open."

I get up from behind the desk and walk around to the front of it. I don't trust myself to get close to her for fear I'll snatch her up and never let go. Instead, I lean back on my desk and fold my arms. "Why?"

She lifts her shoulders, and the scent of her regret agitates me. Or is it pain? Either way, I can't stand it. I want to do everything in the world to change it. "I'm screwing the boss." She sounds sorry, like something sad but inevitable has happened. "This probably won't end well for me."

I narrow my eyes, not liking any of this. "That's pretty fatalistic, isn't it?" I beckon her to me, desperate to touch her, to have her scent closer, but still not trusting myself not to throw her over my shoulder and carry her home to mansion row. To tie her to my bed, mark her with my scent and keep her forever.

She comes as bidden, arms wrapped around her middle. I force myself to move slowly when I settle my hands on her waist, dislodging her hold of it.

"I don't want to lose you."

She blinks those long, curled lashes at me.

"I also don't want to stop..." –It seems to crass and reductive to say *fucking you*– "...this."

She says nothing, just sways unsteadily on her feet, her gaze searching mine.

"What would it take to make this work for you?"

Her lips part, but no sound comes out. She has that frightened look she gets right before she comes. But then it's over. It passes. She shakes her head. "Nothing. I mean, this works for now." She drops her gaze. "I'm just exploring options in case that changes."

Fuck.

"You saw Eleanor Harrington, didn't you? Did she offer you a job?"

"No. She left it open. I made it plain I wasn't actively looking."

"Do you know who she is, Madison?" The softness of my tone makes Madison go still. I've been debating telling Madison about this ever since Sully presented me with the information, but I wasn't sure if it benefitted her. Leaving her in the dark isn't a kindness, though.

"What do you mean?"

"I noticed her interest in you at the ball." I pull her closer. "I also observed what I thought was a family resemblance." It's only a half-lie. I smelled the resemblance.

Madi's brows drop. "What?"

"I asked Sully to look into it, and it seems I was right.

She's most likely your paternal grandmother. She secretly got your mother the job at Landhower Prep and funded your education there. She also ensured your admission to Princeton and–"

"No." Madison cuts me off. "Wait. What are you talking about? You hired a PI? What is this?"

"Her son, Brett Harrington, was in college with your mother. They dated briefly, breaking up eight months before you were born."

"Christ." Madi's face goes pale. "I think I'm going to be sick." Tears brighten her eyes.

"Come here, beautiful." I pull her against my body in an embrace. "I'm sorry it's a shock. I was debating how to tell you."

I sense her belly shudder like she's holding in a sob. I drop my lips to her silky hair and cradle the side of her head to press it against my chest.

"I...*hate* that," she sputters in typical Madi fashion, pushing away. When I release her, she merely repositions herself to lean against my body sideways, crossing her arms. "I hate everything about it."

"You mad at me?"

"No, I'm just–" she paces away from me. "I just hate it." She whirls and spreads her hands. "Why in the hell did she wait until now to make contact? Ugh!" She grimaces. "Don't answer that. I'm sure I know."

I cock my head, not certain what she thinks she knows.

"She was waiting to see how I turned out. Whether I was worthy to claim. Or something sick like that." The tears never fell, and Madi's already composed herself in that surprising way she has of quickly mastering her emotions. "And what about my dad?" She shakes her head. "I guess he's the real asshole here." She stares at me for a moment then visibly gathers herself. "I'm sorry. This isn't your problem. Thanks for the information."

"I'll give you the file my PI put together." I walk around my desk to pull the manila envelope from a drawer.

She takes it and spins on her high heel for the door.

"So you're not quitting me for her?" I ask mildly as she reaches it.

She sends me a look over her shoulder that probably isn't meant to look sexy but goes straight to my cock. "Not in this lifetime."

"Good," I mutter, but she's already out the door, her spine straight, shoulders back as she departs.

My female may be human, but she's as strong and resilient as they come.

Of course, she's not *my* female.

As I walk around my desk, my wolf growls at that mental pronouncement. He wants her. Twenty-four hours a day he's driving me in her direction. To mark her. To claim her. To keep her.

As impossible as it may be, it's hard for me to deny the pull. The attraction isn't just sexual, either. I can't blame it on pheromones and my wolf. I find everything about Madison Evans fascinating. She has all the qualities of an alpha female–if only she were a wolf.

She's capability-porn in motion. Brilliant. Well-spoken but sassy. She's not dramatic or particularly manipulative, but she does manage to get her way. When she doesn't, she handles it with more grace than anyone I've ever seen.

I'm falling in love with her.

I drop into my chair.

Fell. It's already in motion. My heart's in play.

My executive team is right. This problem with the assistant has gotten out of hand. Way out of hand.

Yet, I can't find it in me to pull back.

Every cell in my body screams for me to just move forward. Claim the girl with her inferior genes. Make her mine, even though it could mean losing everything–my position as alpha, even my pack.

Madi

I compartmentalize for a few hours, focusing on the fires that need to be put out around the office, then I pick up the phone to call my mom.

Her last class ends at four, so she should be available to pick up. "Hi, sweetheart!" she exclaims, like she's shocked that I called. A stab of guilt hits me for being so engulfed in my job that I haven't called her at school in weeks. "What's going on?"

"Well, I'm still at work. I had lunch with Eleanor Harrington today."

"What?" The shock in my mom's voice is all I need to confirm Brick's suspicions. "I'm sorry, who did you say?"

"Eleanor Harrington. Do you know her?"

"Uh, well...I've met her once or twice. She's one of the donors at Landhower."

"Yes. I understand she was the donor who funded my education there."

"Did she tell you that?" I sense a note of hysteria in my mom's voice.

"No." I don't say any more. I know from all the books I've read on interrogation and negotiation, the less you say, the more power you hold.

"What did she tell you?"

"Who is she, Mom?"

There's a pause. "What do you mean?"

"Who is Brett Harrington? What do I need to know here?"

"Maybe you should come over for dinner tonight." My mom sounds defeated. "I can answer all your questions."

"I can't come tonight," I snap. "I have the company holiday party. I need the answers now, Mom. Please. I *really hate* when I don't have a full picture, especially when it comes to my own life."

"It sounds like you already know, Madi. What do you want me to say?"

I fling my free hand in the air in exasperation. "Give me the abridged version. Just some concrete facts."

"Okay." She draws in an audible breath. "Brett Harrington is your dad. I met him at Oxford when I was there for my PhD. When I told him I was pregnant, he asked me to get an abortion. I refused, and we broke up. Eleanor flew out and paid me a visit. She offered me a large sum of money if I would end the pregnancy. I told her to go fuck herself. She got nasty–threatened to get me thrown out of Oxford through her contacts there. I decided if the Harrington's were so eager not to be associated with us, I didn't want any part of them. I called Brett–your sperm donor–and told him I'd miscarried, and he didn't need to worry about the baby. He never followed up, but his mom wasn't so easy to get rid of. So we came to an agreement."

Nausea rolls over me again. "What was the agreement?"

"She paid off my student loans and gave me a lump sum in exchange for my signature on papers relinquishing all rights to any Harrington inheritance or paternity suits. I don't know if it would actually hold up in a court of law, but I wanted nothing to do with that vile family after that. I figured we were better off without them."

I blink back tears. "Yeah. Agreed. But you let her pay for my education?"

"I didn't realize she was the one pulling strings at first. By the time I did, you were already a sophomore. You didn't like it socially, but you were excelling so much academically, I couldn't bear to pull you out. I talked to you about it, remember? You wanted to stay because you could take six AP classes a semester there. You loved the challenge."

She's right. I did. Academic success was a new game for me then. I loved pushing myself to see how far and fast I could go. "I remember."

"I've debated telling you, but I wasn't sure it would do anything but hurt you."

"Yeah. I get that. Knowing does hurt."

"I'm sorry, baby. I really am. They're classist assholes. She has no right to contact you now. What—she waited to see how you turned out, and now that you're a Princeton grad working on Wall Street, you're good enough? That's a steaming pile of bullshit, as far as I'm concerned."

My mom doesn't usually resort to cursing, and I suddenly want to hug her. The Harringtons' assholery affected her far more than it has me. I was oblivious to the rejection, while she had to live with it and hide it from me all these years.

"It's fine. But you're right. That's exactly the score."

After a moment of silence, my mom asks, "What are you going to do?" The fact that she sounds scared—like she might lose me to these assholes—guts me.

"I'm going to tell her to go fuck herself," I say although it's more for my mom than for me.

My mom lets out an audible breath.

"I love you, Mom."

"Oh, Madi." She's choked up. "I love you so much. I'm sorry if this hurt you."

"I'm fine. I'm sorry it hurt you. I have to go, but let's do dinner tomorrow?"

"Yeah, I'd like that. Bye, sweetie."

Chapter Ten

Brick

I overheard Madi's conversation with her mother and gave her space in case she needed to process things. At six, I summon her to bring my tux in from the closet. I had some foolish idea about changing in front of her–remembering how turned on she'd been that second week when she'd spilled water on me and walked in when I had my shirt off.

Screwing her in the office has taken the edge off, but it's not the same as taking a female to bed. I don't get to see her naked. There are things I want to do to her that take more time than a quickie stolen during work hours.

Fuck. Me.

She comes in wearing the dress she wore to the charity ball. Of course–it's not like she has another gown. We've already established that. But its effect on me is immediate and painful.

"Oh, honey. You made a huge tactical error wearing that dress again." I've taken off my jacket, tie, and dress shirt, so

I'm standing in my undershirt. I eat up the way her gaze traces where my biceps pop out of the sleeves.

I expect a sassy response, but her expression flickers to doubt, and she freezes in place. "I did?"

I take the tuxedo bag from her and toss it on a chair. "You did." I pick her up and sit her on my desk.

"Jesus, you are strong." She grabs onto my arms and squeezes, like she's testing the muscles. Same thing she did that day she pretended she was blotting the water from my abs.

"Uh huh." I lower my head and trail my tongue lightly around the V of her window, delving between her perky breasts. "You left me with blue balls the last time you wore this, and I haven't forgiven you for it."

She spreads her thighs wide, encouraging me closer. "You haven't?" Her voice is husky and sweet.

"No, Windows. Punishment is definitely in order."

Her pupils dilate. Breath quickens. The scent of her arousal drugs me.

I drop my hands to her hips. "I don't appreciate being teased, little girl. Not at all. So now you're going to feel the sting of your boss' ruler."

"Oh." She sits up taller like she just squeezed her ass. She's adorably aroused, and I'm already desperate to satisfy her, my wolf starting to run the show.

I lean down to murmur the next order right against the shell of her ear. "Go and get it from my desk drawer."

When I step back, she slides off the desk and wobbles to the other side of the desk to open my drawer. Her hand trembles a little when she hands it to me, but I read far more excitement than nerves in her.

"Come back over here." I tap the surface of the desk. She toddles back, and I push her face down over it. I take my time sliding the smooth red fabric of the dress up her legs. "Beautiful girl," I murmur, admiring the shape of her legs, the curve of her ass.

She's in one of her G-strings–the one I already acquainted myself with this morning. I peel it off her, kissing down the back of one leg when I squat to detangle it from her ankles.

I make a detour on my way back up to grip both her thighs and spread them open, so I can lick her sweet pussy. It's an activity I haven't had nearly enough time to indulge in and will never tire of. I work her soft folds until she's moaning, inner thighs quivering, and then I stand.

She lets out a whimper of disappointment.

"Did you think I was going to let you come, Madi-girl? I'm not."

She whirls to look over her shoulder, her silky bob swishing at the sharp action.

"This is punishment, little girl."

"Not listening." The warble in her voice tells me she's hanging on every word.

I take my time picking up the ruler with one hand as I stroke a circle around her ass with the other. "Ready for your spanking?"

"Does anyone ever say yes to that?" Sassy, as always.

I slap the ruler against one of her cheeks, and she gives a little yelp. "The correct answer is yes, sir." I slap the other cheek. "But to answer your question, I wouldn't know. I told you before, you're the only assistant I've had in this particular position."

"I better be," she mutters.

I deliver another spank to each of her cheeks. She gasps and tightens her ass. "Let's try this again." Two more slaps. The ruler leaves delightful red stripes on her cheeks that satisfy my wolf. I'm leaving a mark on her–just not the permanent one he wants me to. "Are you ready for your spanking?"

"Yes, sir." She lets out the words with a light gust of laughter. "And also–*ow*."

I stop and rub the stripes. "Too much?"

"No." Her answer has that soft quality she takes on when she's telling some truth about herself she wasn't sure she wanted to reveal. I've come to love this particular sound from her. Especially because I don't hear it that often.

I decide perhaps the ruler is too much, though. Madison loves sexual dominance, but I don't think she's a pain slut. I use my hand instead, delivering a flurry of spanks that make her gasp and jerk. When I've turned her ass pink, I stop and rub again.

"That's for wearing this dress to a work function. I'm going to be gritting my teeth all night over the fact that men you work with are seeing you in it."

"You're the only man I work with," she reminds me, which gives me a small measure of satisfaction.

I trail my finger along the cleft of her ass until my fingertip comes in contact with the little pucker of her back hole. "I still haven't taken you here." I circle it lightly.

She squeezes it closed. "I-I don't think tonight's, um, the right night–"

My laugh interrupts her. I kick her feet wider. "Agreed. The office doesn't seem like the right place. Which brings me to my next complaint." I give her pussy a light spank, and she gasps. "I need you naked. And in a bed."

I spank her pussy again, and she shivers. I deliver a series of short, light spanks to her clit, my fingers meeting wetness with each slap.

She doesn't offer me a response. No refusal, but no acceptance, either.

I unbutton my trousers and free my Washington Monument-sized erection. "And that's why you don't get to come tonight."

"What?" She tries to straighten, but I hold her down.

"You heard me." I drag the head of my cock through her juices. "I'm not satisfied with your performance, Madison. I'm docking your pay." I ease in.

A frustrated laugh tumbles from her lips. "Are you paying me in orgasms?"

"Not tonight." I feed every inch into her tight channel, then ease back and press forward again.

"Brick!"

I chuckle at her shocked protest because she doesn't use my first name often. It's sweet to hear it now. When I start to move inside her my eyes roll back in my head at the relief. The ecstasy. This is exactly where I need to be. Right now. Every day. Every moment of every day. This is the only time I get a break from the constant pressure my wolf applies.

I take my time, savoring every stroke. Closing my eyes and breathing in her Frankincense and orange scent. I register every sensation acutely. The sound of her panting breaths. The squeeze of her internal muscles around my dick. The slide of her body across my desk.

Soon the sensations overwhelm me. It's too much. I can't wait any longer. I wrap an arm around her waist, so I don't bruise her hips against the wood and buck hard against her soft ass, thrusting deep.

"Don't come, Madison," I warn as I pick up the tempo.

"I will."

My beautiful, disobedient assistant. She rests on her

forearms, her hair swinging forward and back with each brutal thrust.

"Madison." I use my stern boss voice. Heat flushes every inch of my skin. My quads tighten and jerk. Balls draw up. "Do. Not. Come."

"Or what?" She wants a consequence.

I adlib, trying to think of something she might care about. "Or I won't let you go to the holiday party."

I hear her scoff of injustice, and I know I picked the right threat. She whimpers and lowers her head to the desk, holding very still, like she's forcing herself not to enjoy it.

I smile, thrusting hard, on the verge of reaching completion.

My wolf tries to hold me back, pissed that I'm not satisfying the female he believes is our mate. It takes me another moment to work through that block, but when I come, it's incredible. Fireworks explode outside the window. Or maybe just in my mind. Alpha power pours from me into her, like my wolf is trying to anoint her with my essence. Mark her as mine in a different way.

She whimpers again, like she's in pain.

I don't feel like gloating or reminding her that this is how I will feel all night with her walking around in that dress.

No, I simply can't take it. Her pain is mine.

"Good girl." I reach around the front of her hips and find her clit. I touch it very lightly. "You can come now, beautiful." I breathe the words against her ear.

She whimpers one more time and squirms, seeking release. I increase the pressure on her clit, making a tiny circle around it, and she comes–hard. Her muscles squeeze my cock and wring a second mini-orgasm out of me.

I stay buried inside her for a few moments, and she

collapses over the desk, her cheek pressed against the polished wood.

"You are magnificent." I stroke the hair back from her face.

She lets out a laugh. "I think you did all the work there, Big Bad."

I ease out of her and clean her with some tissues.

She turns and rests her hands on my chest. "But it's nice to earn some rare praise from the boss."

I lower my head and kiss her, feeling better now that I've marked her with my essence. Like I might be able to function tonight at the party.

Her stomach growls, and I jerk away. "You're hungry."

"How did you even hear that? I only felt it." She stoops to pick up her panties. "There will be food at the party. Are you going to let me go now?"

"You're going with me."

"Mmm hmm. Got that memo. Can we go soon?"

I move to put on the tuxedo. She pulls on her panties then leans against the desk to watch me change.

"Do you think Jerry knows I'm screwing the boss?"

I want to lie to her, only because I don't want her to feel any shame. But I'm not a liar. And with her brains, she just needs the facts of a situation to figure some angle with it. She should have been an attorney.

I meet her gaze across the room with a rueful twist of my lips. "Probably."

The real answer is definitely. Jerry is a shifter. He smells everything that goes on in this office. He empties our trash. He has shifter hearing, and he's outside the door cleaning right now. He probably heard her ask the question.

She nods.

"Do you mind?"

She turns away from me, so I can't read her face. "Eh. It is what it is, I guess." She walks to the door. "I need to power down my laptop."

I button up my crisp white tuxedo shirt trying to identify the sense of dissatisfaction that's still around despite assuaging my wolf's appetite for Madison a moment ago.

It seems the sex is no longer enough for me.

I want all of Madison. I want to know what's going on in her head. More than that, I want her to share it with me, to confide, to show me her real feelings. This habit she has of buttoning it all up is getting under my skin.

Outside my door, I hear her ask Jerry if he's going to the party. I bare my teeth, a wolf-snarl rising up in my throat at the mere fact she's talking to another male. *In that dress.*

A male who is absolutely no threat.

Even so, I barrel out my door and cast Jerry a dark look, which he immediately heeds by moving swiftly away from behind Madison's desk.

Why in the fuck was he so close to her, anyway?

I stalk over and take Madison's hand, the seething not abating until I have her safely in the elevator.

Fuck me. I will not survive this night.

Madison

I swear Blackthroat was jealous of me talking to the janitor back at the office. He got grumpy and barely said a word on the ride over to the hotel. The horrible weather matches his dark mood. It's snowing that heavy, wet precipitate that makes him keep the windshield wipers at full speed.

The idea that Brick Blackthroat might feel threatened

by a sixty-year-old janitor is so ludicrous, it's laughable. I guess he really does feel territorial of me when I wear this dress. I wish that didn't satisfy me so much. I wish I wasn't rapidly falling for this man. Because I could definitely get used to this. The more time I spend with Brick, the more time I want to spend with him, which is a problem. Because I am terrified of falling off the cliff. I don't want to end up like my mom—in love with some rich guy who is just sowing his wild oats before he settles down with some socialite who fits the family pedigree.

Blackthroat uses valet parking, and it seems we're right on time. The ballroom Moon Co rented is rapidly filling, with festive employees dressed in gowns and tuxes streaming in. The banquet hall is tastefully decorated, and a string quartet plays pop tunes in one corner. That was Genevieve's idea. I guess she's a *Bridgerton* fan or something. I personally think it's a touch stuffy, but what do I know? I'm not from the same social sphere as most of these people.

A waiter walks by with a tray of canapes, and Blackthroat summons him over then indicates it's for me. I pick one and pop it in my mouth.

"Hold up," Blackthroat demands as the waiter starts to move away. "She's hungry."

"Oh." I let out an embarrassed laugh and scoop two more hors d'oeuvres off the tray. "It's true, I am. Thanks."

I spot various members of the executive team looking as at-home and devastatingly handsome in their tuxedos as they did at the last ball, only this time they each have a gorgeous woman on their arm.

"I want you to stay by my side tonight," Blackthroat declares after I knock his hand away from the small of my back. "I will need that memory of yours."

It's bullshit, and we both know it. "This is not a working event. I should be allowed to enjoy the party, same as any other employee."

"Nice try, Windows. I already told you that you're my representative here. Which means I need you by my side."

He really is jealous of other men seeing me in this dress. It's confirmed when I sign hello to Noah across the room, and Blackthroat actually shakes his head at him to warn him from coming over. He tries to put his hand on my back again.

I sidestep away. "What if I want to dance?" I don't. Dancing isn't my forte. I'm just messing with him.

"You'll dance with me."

"Not happening."

"Madison."

My nipples bead up because he's using his stern reprimand-y voice. "Yes?" I keep my tone cool, even though I'm giggling inside.

"You'll stay by my side, or I will toss you over my fucking shoulder and spank your ass as I carry you out."

My knees buckle and panties dampen. Somehow, Brick senses it and places a steadying hand at my elbow. His nostrils flare like he's breathing in my scent.

"No touching," I tell him.

Twenty feet away, I see Billy, who has a stunning but bitchy-looking blonde on his arm. He turns his head and frowns, as if he heard me and didn't like it.

Brick makes a sound of frustration but drops my elbow.

"I'm going to let Genevieve know you're here. She wants you to take the stage and welcome everyone to kick the night off."

"We're staying for thirty minutes, and then we're gone."

"I'm not leaving with you, bossman. It's simply not

happening. And I will stay as long as I want." I cut away to find Genevieve, not looking back to see how Blackthroat took that.

This thing with Brick is getting out of hand. I'm losing control, and I don't like that feeling.

I find Genevieve to deliver the information, and while she and Blackthroat take the stage, I make a beeline for the open bar.

"You know what happens to secretaries who fuck their bosses?" I instantly recognize the condescending voice beside me. I think I'll start calling Billy *Draco Malfoy* behind his back.

I turn and blink at him. "What?" I ask with my business-polite voice.

"Nothing good."

I snort. "Inventive. Did you stay up all night thinking of that zinger?"

The glower he gives me is so hateful it unnerves me, and I have nerves of steel. God, what did I ever do to this guy to earn such spite?

He leans into my personal space. "I'm onto you, Evans. You won't be running that smart mouth when Brick finds out what you're really about." He takes his drink and walks off, leaving me staring.

He's onto me?

What the hell does that mean?

That he knows I'm having sex with Brick? Or does he mean something else?

A sense of misgiving moves through me. I knew when I took this job it would be a hard one to keep. Still, things are different now. Getting fired would mean something went awry between Brick and me. And that...makes my stomach churn.

But I haven't done anything harmful to Moon Co. In fact, I've worked my ass off to make sure its CEO can function at top performance level. Unless you count the time when he's busy making us both come.

I look up to drink in the sight of my boss on the stage. Blackthroat stands beside Genevieve with his hands in his pockets, glowering in my direction. Just the sight of him in that tuxedo, exuding his unique brand of scornful power, weakens my knees.

Brick Blackthroat. My Big Bad Boss. The man dangerously close to luring me in. He takes the microphone from Genevieve, and I have the sudden urge to run.

Very fast.

Away from this event.

It's been too much—finding out about my parentage, getting sniped at by Billy, beginning to want more from Brick.

I need to gather my head.

As my sexy boss offers a curt greeting to his employees, I duck out the door, pick up my coat from the coat check, and get in an elevator. I don't owe him my presence here tonight. Well, I suppose I technically do, but he's not going to fire me over it. My job is now too entwined with sex. With our non-relationship relationship.

When we blow up, it all blows up, and I doubt it will be over this although it's possible I'm trying to move that date forward every time I rebel against him.

I step out of the elevator and debate how to get home. Considering the weather and my attire, I probably need a cab. The doorman holds the door for me, and I step out.

"Taxi?"

"She's going with me," Brick snarls from behind us.

I whirl to see his eyes flashing a strange shade of amber

in the light. He reaches a hand for my hip in a possessive gesture as he thrusts his valet ticket at the attendant.

For some reason, none of my usual snappy responses come to mind. I'm too tired. My brain is churning too much on the Harringtons and my mom and the fact that everyone at Moon Co knows I'm screwing the boss. I'm in limbo–I need to make a decision about this job and Blackthroat, but I keep putting it off because of this. The way I feel every time he demonstrates his interest in me.

I'm hungry for his attention, his affection, his constant approval. I don't want to give up hearing him growl "good girl" or ordering me around in that bossy way of his and watching as I perform for him. I don't want to end the game we play because it's so damn satisfying.

I expect a dressing down about leaving the party, but instead, he modulates his temper for once. Even though I see frustration in the set of his mouth, his voice is a mild rumble. "I'll take you home, Windows."

"I can take a cab."

"It's snowing, I'm taking you home."

I muster a retort. "Newsflash, Big Bad, outside of the office, you're not the boss of me." My words lack my usual snappy delivery, and he must see it because his often flinty gaze is soft on my face.

"Keep telling yourself that, Madison," he murmurs.

* * *

Brick

Something's off with Madison, and it kills me. Was she running from me? Or was it something Billy said to her? I will tear him apart if he hurts her. Literally. With my wolf fangs.

Or maybe this is about that bitch, Eleanor Harrington.

I know Madison has issues with money and social class that likely stem from the situation with her father. This probably poked all those wounds.

She ends up getting into my car without a fuss, but she's miles away.

"Did Billy say something to you?" I ask as we drive.

Her gaze slides my way. "I'm not afraid of Billy."

I reach out and cup the back of her head, massaging her scalp lightly there. "You're not afraid of anyone, are you, Windows?"

She steals another glance at me, as if surprised by the praise.

"Tell me what he said."

She shrugs. "He just said nothing good happens to secretaries who fuck the boss."

I grind my teeth, trying to hold in the growl that rockets up my throat. He's definitely going to feel my wrath. "He will apologize to you on Monday," I grit.

"Don't," she says. "I'm a big girl. I can face the consequences of my actions."

"Nobody speaks to you that way," I snarl then catch the reflection of my gaze in the side mirror and realize my eyes are glowing yellow. I draw in a deep breath to calm myself.

"You'll just make it worse. I don't need you to defend me. I'm fine."

"Talk to me, Madi. Why did you leave the party?"

"It's just been...a day. You know?" Her voice catches, and she turns to me.

I reach for her hand and squeeze it. "Yeah. I'm sorry. What can I do?"

"Nothing."

I hate how immediate and final her response is. I hate

everything about the way this night is going. Instead of dropping her off at her apartment, I drive around the block to find a place to park.

"You don't have to walk me to the door," she says when I miraculously nab a spot a half a block away.

"Invite me up."

"To my apartment?" She lets out an incredulous laugh. "No."

"Then come to my place."

That seems to unnerve her, like sleeping in my bed is far too intimate an act. "Not happening." She flicks open the handle and uses her elbow to push the door open.

I climb out of my side and walk around. "Invite me up."

"I have a roommate–Aubrey, remember?"

"Do you share a bed?"

Another shocked laugh tumbles from her full lips. "Brick..."

I take her hand and walk her to the apartment. "The weather sucks. I don't want to drive back to Central Park."

"You want to spend the night in my apartment." She says it with a note of disbelief, like the mere idea of me staying in Brooklyn is shocking.

Maybe it is. My friends would certainly think I'd lost my mind. This is going far beyond sex with my assistant. We're entering uncharted territory.

But the idea of letting Madi go to sleep alone tonight doesn't sit right with me. I sense the wobble in her world, and I need to hold her through it. Do whatever I can to get her back to her beautiful center. Besides, if she's having a melt-down around money and social status, proving I can sleep in Brooklyn without a fuss might help erase whatever beliefs she might have about the rich being assholes who step on the backs of the poor to stay on top.

She stops in front of the door and searches my face as if trying to understand. "We already had sex twice today."

I take her keys from her hand and open the door. "I'm spending the night, Madi," I say firmly, rather than get into a discussion about whether I do or don't want to feast between her legs and make her scream my name all night long.

Of course, I want that. But I can keep my dick put away if that's not what she needs.

I see the flicker of vulnerability she shows when her armor cracks, and I know I've won.

"It smells like paint," she warns me. "Aubrey is painting a mural in our living room."

"Come on," I coax, nudging her inside and following. "Take me upstairs."

Chapter Eleven

M*adi*

It's all too much.

Not the sex–the sex is amazing. But the implications of Brick being in my apartment.

Aubrey wasn't home when we got in last night, but as Brick brings me to my third orgasm this morning, I hear her moving around the kitchen, softly singing a song by The Cure as she makes breakfast.

Brick clamps a hand over my mouth as I cry out, muffling the sound of my pleasure as he rides to his own.

He was a perfect gentleman last night, helping me out of my dress and drawing me a bath because he decided I was cold.

By the time I got out, I'd warmed up in more than one way, especially after he laid me down on the bed and took his time kissing and licking every inch of my body before he brought me to orgasm. It was incredible.

He's incredible.

That's what has me uneasy. It's the worst part of all of this. I never expected this giving side of Brick. I thought he'd continue to be an asshole, even as a lover, and I was okay with that. It was part of the allure, really. The boss-employee power dynamic turned me on. Like a milder version of master and submissive role play.

But Blackthroat as attentive? Warm, even? The guy who held me all night, lightly brushing circles over my skin every time I stirred?

That I don't even know how to reconcile. Frankly, it terrifies me.

Right now he's like an Adonis in my bed. Naked and gloriously muscled. His eyes reflect golden hues of the morning light as he reaches his peak and slams into me to finish. I wrap my legs around his waist and hook my feet behind him to take him even deeper.

He shudders with pleasure as he releases into me, his strokes turning slow and languid. His lids droop.

What is he even doing here?

In my apartment?

In my bed?

It's a puzzle I can't seem to solve, and I'm the type of person who won't stop worrying a problem until I understand it. Give me an unfinished crossword, and I can't walk away until every box is filled.

But no matter what it is that draws him to me, it won't change the fact that I know he won't stay. Which wouldn't be a problem if it was only about the sex. But it's not that neat and clean.

I could really fall for this guy. Fall hard.

And I know there'd be no cushion to land on when I fall. The billionaire Brick Blackthroat isn't going to put a ring on my finger and walk me down the aisle–not that I think the institution of marriage is the end-all or anything. But regardless. This isn't Cinderella. I don't get the prince.

It's more like *Pride and Prejudice*, except there won't be a happily-ever-after. Falling in love with Brick can only mean one thing: a broken heart.

He takes his fingers away from my mouth and kisses me. "Want to get breakfast?"

"Um." I try to swallow down the lump in my throat. While spending the entire weekend with Brick like he's an actual boyfriend has huge appeal, I just... can't.

It's not the right move to make. It's not smart or practical.

Being with Brick is starting to hurt my heart–I'm falling for him. Not the fantasy of him but the real man. And I know this won't last. It can't. A billionaire from a long line of wealth and status doesn't slum long-term.

I know what I need to do here. "I think you should go," I say. "I need some time to think."

He studies me. "About me?"

My heart flip-flops in my chest. "Yeah," I say softly.

He draws away, his face impassive as he climbs out of the bed and pulls on his undershirt and boxers, then tuxedo pants and shirt, which he leaves unbuttoned. I'm already sorry for pushing him away, even though I know it's the right thing to do.

"Somehow I think you've already made up your mind. Let's have it, Windows."

"I don't think we should have sex any more." I pluck the sheet up to cover my breasts.

He shoves his hands in his pockets and tilts his head. "Odd timing for that pronouncement." His gaze roves over my bare shoulders. "Considering."

Considering he just made me come three times. Yeah, I know. Sue me.

"It's just getting too intense."

139

"Too intense," he echoes hollowly.

"Listen, I like my job," I tell him. "I'd like to keep it. Is, ah, that possible?"

Annoyance flickers over his face. "Of course it's possible, Windows." He stares at me for a moment, revealing nothing of his thoughts, then shoves his feet into his shoes, picks up the tuxedo jacket, and walks out.

Ouch. That...sucked.

"I'm sorry." I speak the flat words to the shut door. He's already gone.

I thought I would feel relieved, especially because I still have the job–which I really have come to love. Instead, an unfamiliar anxiety brews in the pit of my stomach.

Like I made a mistake. And I rarely make mistakes. I'm allergic to them.

A moment later, Aubrey throws my door open and launches onto my bed in her *Women are fragile like a bomb* t-shirt and purple lace panties. "Oh my God! What is wrong with you? I didn't even know Brick Blackthroat was in our apartment. You could've texted or something!"

I fall back on the bed and throw an arm across my face. "I'm sorry! I'm an asshole. Did he see you in your underwear?"

"Well, *yeah!* Not that I care. It just was a shock. I mean, I thought you were going to walk out of your room and instead it's this broad-shouldered billionaire asshole in a tux looking like he just ate a lemon."

"He's not an asshole." I'm surprised at the rush of defensiveness that wells up in me at her dig. "And the lemon-face was because I just told him I didn't want to have sex anymore."

"That seems like odd timing. Did you say it right after doing it?"

I guess she heard.

Aubrey sits on the bed.

"Yes. He found the timing unusual as well."

"So what happened?"

"Nothing. I mean, it was just getting to be too much, you know? Him coming over here and asking me to invite him up. He's not what I thought–he's really not a dick. I mean, he certainly can be, but not to the people he cares about. Like his sister and niece and nephew and..."

Aubrey's dark head pops up from the pillow. "And?"

I try to fight back the irrational sensation of panic rising in my chest. "I don't know!" I throw my hands in the air. "Maybe me!"

Aubrey gives me an exaggerated jaw drop with an extended gasp.

"Stop it."

"You just broke it off because you're afraid he cares about you?"

"Well, no. I mean, yes." I try to organize my thoughts. "No! I broke it off because I care whether he cares, and that's a real problem."

"You know...there are no guarantees in love." Aubrey props her cheek on her hand.

"Please don't."

She laughs. "I'm just saying. You're trying so hard to protect yourself, but is it worth it?"

"There was no *love*! This was my winter fling, remember? And now it's over."

"Okay, that's legit. So did you quit the job, too?"

"No, he said I can keep the job."

"Well, *of course*. He'd better say that, or he'd have a lawsuit on his hands. You can't require a woman to have sex to keep a job. Which I know you know."

"Right." I throw off the sense that I made a mistake along with the covers and climb out of bed, grabbing a shirt to pull over my head, so Aubrey doesn't have to look at me stark naked. "So it's all good. I had some great boss sex and now I'm taking a break. End of story."

"And you could probably always hit that again anytime you wanted to. You know, just for sex-sake. Sex-sake..." she repeats. "I just made up a new word." She grins at me, and a bit of my dark mood lifts.

Not at the prospect of renewing things with Brick. That would be a bad idea. But it's nice to know I could choose it if I really wanted to. That it's still an option. Because Aubrey's right. It's not like I just broke Brick's heart. He didn't even argue with me–he knew it had to end at some point, too. This was just about sex. Things were getting out of that realm, so we needed to take a break. Once the distance has built back up between us, maybe we can indulge again. Not often–just once in a while.

My heart picks up speed at the idea of it not being completely over–further sign that I really *am* in too deep and *can't* manage what we had.

I need to take a breather. Maybe date some other men. Remind myself that Brick is not the kind of guy you dream about keeping.

Not even close.

Chapter Twelve

rick

Bloody prints mar the snowpack all around the Berkshire cottage. I've run until my paws bled for the last two days trying to keep my wolf at bay. He wants blood although it's unclear who I should attack.

Myself for not fighting for Madison? But how would that work? I can't offer her more. I'm not human. I can't buy a diamond engagement ring for the first woman I've slept with who feels like my equal.

Because Madison's *not* my equal. She's a terrible match for me simply because she's a different species. We come from different worlds. She thinks it's because of money and station, but it's far deeper than that.

It's biology.

Culture.

And to be with her, I'd have to forsake my entire family and pack. Something I'm not willing to do.

This termination of our sexual arrangement was inevitable. Probably better it came sooner than later.

My phone rings for the hundredth time. The guys have

been blowing it up. Me leaving the party early wasn't a shocker to them, but not answering their texts asking where I went is out of character. Now it's Sunday night, and they haven't heard from me, so I suspect they're starting to worry. Enough that Ruby called Liz this afternoon to make sure I'm here.

This time it's Billy. Since my wolf wants his blood, I pick up. "What?"

"Is...everything okay?"

I nearly crush my phone. "No, you asshat. I'm going to snap your neck when I see you."

"Okay," he says carefully. "Is this about the secretary?"

The outer case of the phone cracks. *"I told you not to call her that."*

"Madison," he amends. "I'm sorry, Alpha."

"Don't *Alpha* me. You obviously have no shred of respect for me or my position, or you wouldn't interfere in my personal fucking business."

Billy's smart enough to keep his mouth shut. He's lucky we're having this conversation over the phone, or he'd be under my paws right now, bleeding from my fangs.

It gives me a moment to get my wolf's rage back under control.

"You ever speak disrespectfully to her again, and I will cut off your fucking ears."

I mean it.

Of course they would grow right back. Shifters have instant healing properties—another trait that makes us far superior to humans.

"Understood. I will...*apologize*." He says the last word like his mouth is full of thistles.

"You won't go near her again. There's no need. You succeeded in humiliating her, and she ended it."

I'm giving Billy too much credit. She didn't end things because of him, but it gives me a cheap satisfaction to have someone besides myself to blame for it.

Madison has been well-defended from the beginning, and I've done nothing to knock down those walls. Given her nothing. Made her no promises. Of course she broke it off when we started to experience real affection for each other. But what could I offer her?

"Arrange the trip to Sweden for the Winter Pack Games."

"Consider it done." Billy wisely keeps the chortle of glee out of his voice, but I can imagine his triumphant expression. Cock sucker.

It only adds to my piss-off that he was probably right all along. I need to stop wasting my attention on my beautiful assistant and expend every effort to find an alpha she-wolf to mate.

If I don't, I will be consumed by moon madness.

Chapter Thirteen

M *adi*

"Windows." Blackthroat stands in the doorway of his office instead of calling me on the intercom. He's shadow-eyed again today, his expression stamped in a deep scowl. It appears he forgot to shave this morning, or he slept at the office because his jaw is stubbled with more than a five o'clock shadow.

He's truly been on a rampage–firing ten people in the two days he's been back since the weekend. I've heard him slamming and throwing things in his office. Pacing. Raising his voice on the phone. Barking at nearly everyone, including his executive team.

Unbelievably, *none* of his anger has been directed toward me. It's almost like he's purposely walking on eggshells. With me, he's been totally civil–bordering on polite.

I can't quite decipher it. Surely he doesn't believe I would ever file a sexual harassment suit against him. I know I tossed out the notion of me being unfireable after that first time we had sex, but I would never use that against him.

"Yes, sir?"

"Aiden Adalwulf sent me an offer for the Adirondack property. Call him and set up a meeting."

My brows shoot up. "You're selling the property you just bought, sir?"

He tugs at the blue striped tie like it's too tight, even though it's already much looser than he usually wears it. "Tell him this is his one and only chance to buy it. If he brings me a certified check in the mid eight figures this afternoon, I won't sell it to the other bidder."

"Is there another bidder, sir?"

Three months ago I wouldn't dare ask questions about his business. Three months ago, he would have shredded me like confetti for doing so. Now, though, he simply shakes his head. "There is not. I'm sweating him for sport."

He seems to be sweating everyone for sport this week.

My beautiful, sadistic boss.

This version of Blackthroat informed my first impression of the man when I came to work at Moon Co. The heartless, callous, pompous Wall Street CEO out for blood all as a form of entertainment.

Is it weird that in addition to finding it sexy in an anti-hero sort of way, I now find him completely relatable? That's frightening. I probably should get off Wall Street before I become like these people.

"Madison?"

I pause with my hand mid-air, already reaching for the phone to call Aiden. Blackthroat's tie is eskew, and his hair looks like he's been tunneling fingers through it. "Yes, sir?"

"Don't wear those dresses anymore." He doesn't use his bossman voice with me. The words ring as more of an appeal. Friend to friend. "Please. I truly can't take it."

It's an absurd pronouncement, but for some reason, I

believe him. For whatever reason, my billionaire boss seems to actually find *me*–a young woman barely out of college with mediocre sex appeal, and a strong dose of nerd–to be irresistible.

I can't fully digest that information–it makes my head swim. I touch the window cut-out of today's dress. I didn't wear it to taunt him. The dresses have become part of my identity here.

Blackthroat offers a grim smile. "Expense a new wardrobe. Fly to Paris on my dime to shop. Just please stop with the torture."

I can't seem to think of a single response, so I settle for a wobbly nod and "Understood."

He appears almost pained as he turns away. "Thank you."

I draw a breath and pick up the phone to call Adalwulf's office.

His assistant seems to recognize my name. "Yes, Ms. Evans. What can I do for you?"

"I'm calling on behalf of Mr. Blackthroat. He has an eight-figure offer on the Adirondack property, but he's willing to entertain a competing offer from Mr. Adalwulf this afternoon, provided he brings a certified check."

The assistant is silent for a half-beat, then she draws a quick breath. "Will you hold for just a moment, Ms. Evans?"

"Yes."

I wait on hold a full three minutes before she returns and says, "Mr. Adalwulf will send a courier over with an offer this afternoon."

"Oh, I'm afraid Mr. Blackthroat insists that Mr. Adalwulf deliver it personally." I'm not sure if that's true, but Blackthroat wanted to sweat Adalwulf, and I don't care for the guy, so I'm going to represent my boss' interests here.

"Please hold."

Another three minutes passes. "Mr. Adalwulf will bring it personally to Mr. Blackthroat this afternoon."

"May I tell him what time to expect Mr. Adalwulf?"

"I will call when he leaves the office."

"Thank you so much."

She calls close to five. Adalwulf probably thought he was sweating Blackthroat back, but it's not like he was in any position to win anything. Blackthroat has something he wants, and now he has to beg for it.

That has to hurt.

I call Brick via intercom to let him know.

"Get my executive team up here for the meeting," he replies.

I call each of them, and the team streams upstairs looking both gleeful and deadly, like the badass adventure team slow-mo walking away from the explosion.

They're definitely out for blood. I would pity Adalwulf if I weren't so firmly on Blackthroat's side in the matter.

Adalwulf arrives equally padded with courtiers. A half-dozen men enter, all dressed as expensively as their master.

"He's waiting for you in the conference room." I extend a polite arm, like a butler. "It's right this way."

Adalwulf gives me a raking glance, and his nostrils flare on an inhale as he walks by me.

I follow the men into the conference room and stand politely in the doorway. I already set the fancy glass water bottles at every place, but I look at Blackthroat. "May I get you anything?"

His eyes glint that strange golden glow they sometimes take on in the light. "Stay and take notes." That amber gaze meets mine, and I understand what he's asking me.

For some unfathomable reason, Brick Blackthroat finds my presence stabilizing, and he wants me in the room when he deals with his treacherous cousin.

"Of course, sir."

Adalwulf, who is positioned with his back to me, turns with a leer. He seems to think he knows something about me. About us. He appears almost gleeful now.

What was the secret he mentioned to me that night he was waiting outside?

How did he know I'd come home at that time? My brain suddenly snags on the thread and pulls. I don't know why I didn't consider this question at the time. Was he waiting for me? Or was there someone inside the building who told him when I left for the day? Or was he there for another reason?

I find my chair in the corner and sink into it, chewing on this mystery.

"You sure you want her in here for this?" Adalwulf taunts Blackthroat.

My brow furrows.

"I would've thought these negotiations might be kept a bit more private." There's a sneer to Adalwulf's words I don't like. I also don't like not knowing what in the hell he's talking about.

"Did you bring an offer?" Eagle cuts across the tension.

Adalwulf tosses an envelope–literally flicks it through the air–across the table. "I think you'll find it more than adequate," he drawls.

Eagle picks it up, glancing at Blackthroat for approval

before opening the flap and pulling out a note. "What the fuck?"

Red tints his cheeks as he shows it to Blackthroat.

"An offer to take the property off your hands," Aiden says. "For nothing." One of his men sniggers.

"What is the meaning of this?" There's violence in Blackthroat's voice.

The temperature in the room drops twenty degrees.

"A more than adequate offer now that the acreage is fouled with the Blackthroat stench." Aiden glows with the pleasure of delivering the insult. Both sides of the table are glaring at each other so murderously, it's getting hard to breathe.

"How dare you–" Billy starts, but Brick raises a hand, and Billy snaps his mouth shut.

"No," Blackthroat growls, crumpling the paper in his fist. "Nothing will induce me to sell to you now. Nothing short of controlling interest in Adalwulf Associates."

"Controlling interest." Aiden's chuckle sends a frisson of terror down my spine. "Have you grown tired of playing with fake money?" He flicks his fingers, and the way Jake stiffens I know that's a crypto dig. "You must be longing to see how a real company is run."

A tremor runs through Brick, his shoulders tensing so hard, his muscles bulge under his suit. He looks ready to pummel his fist into Aiden's face. But then he seems to get a hold of himself. "I should've known you'd deal in bad faith. You're not really in charge. Your father makes the real moves."

Adalwulf surges to his feet. His henchmen also rise. "My father is not CEO. I am."

"But he does have you on his leash." Blackthroat's smile

is fake and cold. "How does it feel, to be counting down the seconds until your old man croaks?"

I suck in a breath at Blackthroat's heartless attack, but Adalwulf isn't shocked by it. Instead, he narrows his eyes.

"At least he hasn't been poisoned by his own mate. How does it feel to have your beloved mother bring about your entire family's downfall?"

An inhuman roar rips from Blackthroat, and violent chaos erupts. I don't even know what happened, nor how it happened, but I hear the rip of shredded clothing right before something huge and furry hurtles across the table at Adalwulf.

A beast. Some kind of animal.

A wolf.

A giant, tan and black wolf arcing through the air, fangs snapping for Adalwulf's throat.

Everyone surges into action–men shoving back from the table and putting hands on each other's expensive suits.

My scream pierces the air.

The huge wolf turns at the sound of my scream.

"Not here! Not in the boardroom! Are you nuts?" Nickel shouts, shoving one of Adalwulf's men away from him and focusing on Blackthroat.

That's when it finally comes together in my head that the first wolf is Blackthroat. *Brick Blackthroat.* My boss.

He's a wolf. *Werewolf.* Something unnatural and terrifying.

I'm on my feet. I can't seem to stop screaming. My throat hurts with the effort, but I have no control over my reaction. It's like I'm in a horror movie, rooted in place, only able to sound an alarm with my vocal cords.

Someone–Jake, I think–grabs me from behind and claps a hand over my mouth. Later, I would understand he was just trying to shut me up, but I'm in full flight or fight mode, so I wrestle against his hold on me, trying to escape.

Blackthroat wheels between Aiden and me, snarling and showing fangs. His eyes glow amber, unnaturally bright.

Goosebumps rise on every inch of my skin as I remember seeing those eyes on him before. *The eyes of a wolf.*

He abandons Adalwulf, now charging for me. I scream louder. More frantically. This thing is clearly not Blackthroat—it's some feral beast, out of control, and he's going to kill us all.

I struggle against Jake's hold.

"Stop screaming, Madi," Jake growls in a low voice. Somewhere in the back of my brain it occurs to me that Jake seems quite calm considering there's a wild beast coming at us.

Blackthroat leaps, but Jake turns sideways and kicks at the wolf's great jaws, jamming his thousand dollar Louboutin Greggo in the animal's mouth.

"*Brick!* I'm not hurting her," Jake shouts, maneuvering me away from the wolf and kicking at it. "*You* are the one freaking her the fuck out. Change back."

The wolf snarls and lunges again. His fur stands up on his neck and across his broad shoulders. Jake blocks his snapping jaws with another swift kick. "Change back you fucktwat," Jake snarls at the wolf.

"For fuck's sake, Brick," Nickel shouts. "Are you insane?"

Now it fully sinks in. Jake is not surprised that Blackthroat is a wolf. Nor is Nickel. In fact, no one here is surprised by the wolf in the room.

No one but me.

154

There's a snap and crackle of joints, and then suddenly Blackthroat looms before us in human form, completely naked, muscles bulging. "Let go of her!" he roars.

Jake immediately unhands me. "For fuck's sake. I was trying to keep her safe."

I remain frozen another moment, trembling. Taking in the scene in the room.

Across the room, Aiden Adalwulf's eyes glitter silver. He's smiling, showing canines that are a touch too long to be entirely human. *He's one of them.*

The room filled with angry, jostling men in the two camps. All of them are in on the secret I hadn't known. All of them are probably wolves, like their masters.

I take in my naked, beautiful, terrifying boss.

Who is not a human.

A whimper escapes my lips, and every eye in the room fixes on me.

"You *had* to fuck the secretary," Billy mutters bitterly. "Now what are we going to do with her?"

Chapter Fourteen

Brick

Aiden's fangs shrink and his eyes stop glittering as he gets his wolf under control and calmly wipes the blood from his throat, a small smile on his face, like I played right into his hands. Like he loves that I lost control, and he didn't.

I don't give a shit about any of them. Not about the carnage in the room or the weakness I just exposed. Nor about how close I might be to moon madness.

All I care about is Madi. My trembling, terrified dream assistant. The scent of her fear drives my wolf mad. Seeing Jake restraining her made me murderous.

"The Blackthroat king's weakness," Aiden pronounces, studying Madi. He sounds like he's quoting something. *"She will destroy all that he desires."*

Fuck.

I know what he's quoting. It must be a prophecy from that crone wolf-witch in his family. The seeress who has always given the Adalwulf's an advantage in the war between the two packs.

The hairs stand up on the back of my neck.

That's when Madi bolts from the room.

No one dares stop her. They must know I would shred them to ribbons with my fangs if anyone else touched her.

I pause long enough to grab a pair of boxers and pants from the closet and yank them on, then follow. Her scent doesn't lead to the elevator.

Instead, I follow it to the emergency stairwell. I throw open the door, prepared to leap down a flight of stairs at a time, but I find her huddled inside the door, her back against the concrete wall, knees drawn up to her chest. She's panting like she can't catch her breath, holding her head between her knees to keep from passing out. She's in shock.

I force myself to slow my approach to appear non-threatening. "Madi. Sweetheart." I crouch in front of her. "You're safe, Madi. You're always safe with me."

My mind spins on how to help her. What to say. She's not a delicate flower who just needs to be held. No, Madi's a very smart young woman. If she's flipping out right now, it's because she hasn't wrapped her mind around what she just saw. She probably requires facts to assimilate it all.

I sit on the top stair and start speaking softly. "I'm a wolf."

She doesn't answer. I didn't expect her to.

"A shifter. Moon Co is run by shifters. We're not harmful to humans. We're just another species."

She's still sucking in her breath, her shoulder blades jutting out in a way that makes her appear so damn vulnerable.

"I'm not a monster, Madi. I'm just different, that's all." I reach out and touch her knee. "You're safe."

Her breathing slows. She lifts her head from between her knees and gives me a tentative glance.

"This may be a good time to remind you of the NDA you signed." It's meant to be a joke to lighten the mood.

It works. She lets out a weak laugh.

"H-how many?"

Of course she just wants more facts. That's my brilliant girl.

"How many of us are wolves?"

She nods.

I scoot closer to her, still careful not to move quickly. "All of the executive team. Less than a hundred others. Most of my employees are human."

"I mean how many in the world?"

"Oh, percentage-wise? It's very low. Our species are endangered. A fraction of a percent."

"Oh." She rubs the fronts of her legs like she's trying to warm up, but her gaze jumps around like her brain is churning. She gasps, eyes widening. "That's why your name is Blackthroat. Because of the markings on your fur." She brings her fingers to her throat, stroking the place where I have a line of black fur that runs from chin to chest.

"Yes."

"And your cousin is *Adalwulf*. It's so obvious now. Gives a whole new meaning to the Wolves of Wall Street doesn't it?" Her laugh has a hysterical note to it.

"We prefer Werewolves of Wall Street." The corners of my lips lift in a tentative smile.

"The wolves in the Berkshires?"

"My sister and the team out looking for you."

She gives a rueful laugh. "Ruby was the one with the black markings on her throat and chest like yours."

"Exactly."

"She was trying to comfort me."

"Yes." Of course, she's put it all together quickly.

She sits quietly, still chewing on it all, but I sense the fear ebb away. Her scent returns to normal, her breath evens, and she stops trembling and rubbing her shins.

"Are you okay?" I ask after a moment. "May I touch you?"

When she nods, I pick her up and pull her into my lap.

"You're stronger than a human," she realizes. "That's how you make me feel so light."

"You're like a feather to me, Windows."

My wolf's agitation ebbs having her in my arms. Breathing her scent.

If I were honest with myself, I'd admit that Madi breaking things off with me was the reason I lost control back there. My wolf has been way too on edge.

My wolf chose her–a human–to be his mate.

That was the reason for the prophecy from the Adalwulf crone. *She will destroy all he desires.* If I accept Madi as my mate, I will lose everything–my pack, my power. Probably even my business and friends.

But if I don't claim her, I may not physically survive. Moon madness may ravage me. If I go completely feral, they will have to put me down. We'd still lose the pack because Auggie isn't old enough to take the mantle, and the men in my inner circle may not be strong enough to garner pack support. Pack members would defect to the Adalwulf pack.

It's a lose-lose for me, and it's all Madi's fault. Madi and her sweet orange-Frankincense scent and the peek-a-boo dresses. I nuzzle against her shoulder, needing another hit of her scent.

She's still processing. "You don't turn people? It's not a sickness?"

"No, the movies got that wrong. And we don't hunt humans."

She turns to study my face. I don't know what she sees–I try to mask the bald hunger I have for her. The desire to carry her out of here and straight to my penthouse. To tie her to my bed and keep her forever but as a dark secret no one knows.

Of course, I can't do any of those things.

She leans her head against mine. "You're a werewolf. Things are coming together in my mind still. Christ, that really freaked me out, Brick."

"I'll bet. I'm sorry. I can't believe I lost it like that."

She pulls away and runs her fingers around my neck and across my hairy chest. I almost whimper at the pleasure of her touch. "Were you hurt?"

I scoff. "No, sweetheart. I was the one ripping flesh back there. And even if he'd bitten me, we can't get hurt. Shifters heal almost instantly."

"Why...why did you lose it, Brick?"

I can tell by her hesitation that she's asking about *us*. When it's business, she's confident and articulate. But she must suspect she's the cause of my edginess. She's asking for confirmation.

I owe her the truth. I cradle the back of her neck. Rub my thumb lightly over her pulse.

"This secret of mine is why I didn't fight for you when you ended things. But not having you isn't working for me. I've missed you, and I'm cranky as hell, Madi. What happened in there" –I jerk my thumb toward the conference room– "isn't supposed to happen."

She blinks.

I haven't said enough yet. She needs more from me. Or maybe I have it all wrong–maybe Madi never wanted me to fight for her. It could be she's just not that interested.

But I know that's not true. This is the girl who works

161

her ass off to please me. Her body responds to mine—I can tell by her scent. She cares. She just doesn't want to care.

And that's because she's afraid. Her father's abandonment of her family because of their social status left a scar. My position and money make me seem similar. I need to make her understand I'm not.

"I'm different from you, Madi, but not in the way you thought. It's not about our income or social status difference, it's plain biology. If you felt like my team disapproved, it's only because relationships between shifters and humans are frowned on, especially for an alpha."

Understanding dawns on her face. "You're the alpha."

"Yes."

"Of...a *pack*?"

"Yes."

"Is the pack Moon Co?"

"Well, the pack is simply a community of shifters, but yes, many of my pack members work here."

"And Aiden...?"

"His father is alpha of their pack. My parents were from rival packs. A regular Romeo and Juliet."

Her eyes round.

"In light of that relationship, ours can hardly be worse. Listen, Madi—" I kiss the bare skin framed by the cut-out of her dress. "A relationship with a human might be difficult, but I'd like to explore it with you."

Madison takes in a sharp breath and holds it.

"Wolves aren't usually attracted to humans, but I'm helplessly, hopelessly attracted to you. When you called it quits, I tried to shake it off, but I can't. You're all I want."

She blinks rapidly like she's hiding tears. "Oh."

"Come home with me tonight," I coax, biting her breast through her dress. "I need to have you near me. Please."

The scent of her arousal floods my nostrils, making me dizzy with lust.

She gives a tiny nod of assent. "Okay." Her answer is sweet and soft.

It's everything I need to hear.

Chapter Fifteen

Madi

Brick Blackthroat wants to have a relationship with me. That almost shocks me more than the fact that he's a wolf. I'm still quickly assimilating both as Brick drives me to his place.

When we left the stairwell, hand-in-hand, the Adalwulf contingent had already vacated the building, and it was just Blackthroat's team left in the conference room, discussing the situation in heated voices.

The way they all stopped talking when we came in tells me I was a large part of that discussion.

"What now?" Vance asked in a tight voice, his gaze flicking from me to Blackthroat.

"Go home. I'll clean up my own mess."

None of them seemed to like that, but other than disgruntled stares, no one protested.

"Am I your mess?" I ask as we drive. "When you said you'd clean up your own mess, did that mean me?"

He slides a sidelong glance at me from behind the

wheel. "Humans aren't supposed to know about our kind. Obviously."

"Yes, obviously." I'd already assumed that much. "As you said, I signed an NDA. I won't breathe a word. Not even to Aubrey."

He sends me another unfathomable glance. "Thank you."

I fidget for another moment. I have to ask. "Are you taking me home because I'm part of the mess?"

"No, Windows." He gives a humorless laugh. "I would have your memory wiped if I didn't trust you—without hesitation. Even though it could damage that big, beautiful brain of yours. We take our privacy and pack safety very seriously."

A shiver runs down my spine. I don't want to know the answer, but I have to ask. "H-how?"

"I'd make a deal with Thaddeus, the vampire king. Vampires can fuck with minds. Hypnotic suggestions and all that."

The shiver turns into a shudder. "Okay. Wow. Vampires exist, too."

He reaches out and squeezes my hand like he did in the stairwell. "You're safe with me, Madison. Do you believe that?"

I draw in a breath, considering. The connections are still coming together in my mind as I sort through all of our past interactions. When I view them through the lens of Brick being a werewolf, they make more sense. The weird rules about no fragrances in the building. The prohibition against silver. His reaction to having me show up in the Berkshires and spending Thanksgiving with the pack. The protectiveness of everyone around him.

I see what Blackthroat meant. It was never about our

social status difference. I thought that because of my own hang ups with money, but it was a werewolf-human thing. I'm an outsider getting too close.

So am I safe with him?

Yes, I think I am.

His behavior toward me points only toward a steady and continued interest in me. He's not dragging me off to his place now to make me his wolf-dinner. Or turn me into one of his kind. Or even mind-wipe me with a vampire. I know when he's lying. He does that overly-scornful act.

Besides, why would he tell me about the vampire thing if he planned to use it on me?

"Yes," I answer him out loud. "Why are we going to your place?"

This time there's no mistaking the meaning behind his look. It's positively feral. "Because, Windows, I haven't feasted between your legs in over four days, and it's absolutely killing me."

I squirm in my seat.

Brick's nostrils flare. "I can smell your arousal, sweetheart. Good thing we're here." He drives into an underground parking garage with a manned gate. The security guard waves to Blackthroat as he drives through. After a spiral downward we go through a few more gates–these automatic–and enter what appears to be a luxury car showroom. The spotless floor is coated in a gleaming pale silver epoxy, the ceiling has ultra-modern recessed light banks. A few dozen gorgeous cars worth eight figures each fill the parking spaces.

"What...where are we?"

"My garage."

I barely hold in my gasp. "Your...*personal* garage?"

"Yes. But a lot of these cars belonged to my father."

I'm dying. Literally dying. I'm not a car person, but if I were, I'd probably orgasm right here. There are Jaguars and Astin Martins, Porsches and limousines. New models. Old ones. All in mint condition. "Gulp."

Brick walks around to take my hand when I get out. "Did you just say *gulp?*" He pushes me against a shiny red Ferrari and insinuates one muscular thigh between my legs.

"Yes."

"Get used to my money, Windows."

I confess to being a little drugged by his dominance. His pushing me up against the car and molding his body against mine has me breathless. So I blink up in confusion. "What?"

"You have a hang-up with money. A chip on your shoulder."

"*I* have a chip?" I sputter.

His grin makes him look boyish. The way his hands roam inside the coat he bought me makes me squirm, and I rub my needy clit against his thigh wedged between my legs. "You definitely have issues with it." He lowers his head and nibbles at my neck. "I want to spoil you with my money. Will you let me?"

Oh my *gawd*. It's not dirty talk. I mean, I'm sure he doesn't mean it to be, but everything in me electrifies at his words. My nipples turn as hard as diamonds, my core clenches. As much as he's right–I do have hang-ups with his money–this request, delivered in Brick's demanding, bossy way, nearly makes me come.

He wants to spoil me with his money.

I have parameters and definitions about money. I want to earn it. Legitimately. Through my hard work and brains. I don't want it given to me. I resent people–like the Black-

168

throats–who had it handed to them without hard work or earning it.

I didn't like finding out Eleanor Harrington paid for my secondary education or that I may have gotten financial assistance from Princeton through her connections.

But something about Brick's request blows all my armor around money off. Strips me bare. Spreads my legs and demands I receive.

"M-maybe." I'm trembling again, only this time it's not from fear.

"Are you cold, sweet girl?" In a flash, I find myself up in Brick's arms. I guess now that he doesn't have to hide his superior strength, he can show off a little. I loop my arms around his neck, letting out a breathy laugh.

He carries me to an elevator, which seems to have a thumbprint recognition because after he presses his thumb, a crisp, computerized voice says, "Welcome, Mr. Blackthroat," and the doors swish open.

"Oh my God!" I laugh.

He must hear some judgment in my astonishment because he says, "You're hard to impress, you know that, Madison?"

I think that guts me more than anything. Has Blackthroat been trying to impress me and thought he'd failed?

Far from it.

So very far.

"I just hide it well. I'm not immune to your many charms, Big Bad. I just pretend I am."

"I'm not sure I've been called charming before." Another thumbprint recognition zips us up in the elevator, and the doors open to a short hallway leading to a single door. The penthouse is a beautiful space–brick walls and hardwood floors. Wall-to-wall windows overlook Central

169

Park. The ceilings are lofted with exposed fixtures and pipes. It somehow manages to be both warm and industrial at once. Masculine but refined. There are Persian rugs on the floors, and the furniture is a mix of antique and modern.

"I think you're purposely anti-charming," I accuse as he strides through the living room and takes me straight to the bedroom—which also features floor-to-ceiling windows overlooking the park and a giant king bed in the middle of the room.

"Definitely."

"Can dinner be a part of tonight's activities?" I ask when I realize his plan. It's past eight, and I'm starving.

He stops, closing his eyes as if he's angry with himself for forgetting. Either that or he's mustering control. "Of course. I'm so sorry."

"Trophy," I mutter.

He chuckles. "I'll order some food to be brought up. I *really* need to get you naked right now." He tosses me effortlessly into the middle of the bed, and I shimmy out of my coat and kick my heels onto his rug. "But I do want to take you out soon. For dinner. For lunch. To Paris. Rome. Milan. May I court you, properly, Madison Evans?"

I try to breathe through the giddiness. This can't all be true. He's way too Prince Charming. And I'm way too Cinderella.

He tilts his head when I don't answer.

"Yes, sir?" I offer with a smile.

"Oh, are we doing the *sir* thing?" He never put a tie back on after shifting, but he produces one from his pocket now.

I suddenly understand why he keeps changes of clothes at the office. In case he spontaneously shreds his suit changing into wolf form.

"Okay, Windows. I'll give you what you need from your Big Bad Boss." He snaps the tie between two hands like he's showing me a belt, then rolls me to my belly and pins my hands behind my back.

I laugh and kick my feet, creaming my panties when he winds the tie around my wrists and secures them.

"That should hold you while I order food and then take my time turning this ass pink." He slides both hands up the backs of my thighs, dragging the hem of my dress with them.

I moan softly, soaking the gusset of my G-string.

Brick leans over and bites one cheek as he strokes the other with a light caress.

"Ooh!" I squeal.

He continues to trail his fingertips over my ass while he pulls out his phone and calls a restaurant. "Brick Black-throat speaking," he says gruffly.

"Mr. Blackthroat. What can I do for you?" I hear the simpering reply.

"Send over an order of all your specials today and bill it to my card on file with a hundred dollar tip."

No wonder they simper. Blackthroat may bark a lot, but he's not ungenerous.

"How many entrees total, Mr. Blackthroat?"

"I don't care. There are two of us, but I want to be sure there's something she likes, so send a variety."

"Absolutely. Right away, sir."

The moment he ends the call—at least I hope he ended it—his hand claps down on my ass, making me startle and gasp.

"I'm going to make you regret stonewalling me, little girl," he growls, slapping the other side.

"Did you say something?" I tease because I don't answer to *little girl*.

171

He delivers a flurry of hard spanks, and I kick and squeal. "Don't pretend your nipples don't get hard every time I call you that." He rubs a circle around my ass, then slides his fingers under my panties to rub between my legs. "But what would you prefer? Babygirl? Little one? HILF?"

"Human you'd like to fuck?

"Human I *love* to fuck." He peels my G-string down and off my legs. "HINF. Human I *need* to fuck." He lifts my hips up until I'm resting on my knees with my ass in the air, my face pressed into his luxurious grey down comforter. He palms my ass and licks into me from behind, making me scream into the covers.

He tortures me with a slow roll of his tongue around my clit, then a circuit around all my folds. "Fates, I missed that taste." He nips and kisses my inner thighs, my labia, my entrance. The stubble on his face chafes the delicate skin, adding to the heat he delivered when he spanked me.

My belly shudders in and out, my inner thighs tremble. My arms are starting to ache from being pinned behind my back. "I'm ready," I murmur.

"Ready for what?" Brick bites the back of my thigh, and I warble.

"I don't need more foreplay. I mean, if you want to–"

I hear the zipper on Brick's trousers. "You don't have to ask me twice, sweetheart. I need to get between those legs like I need my next breath."

He isn't kidding. Within three seconds, he's impaled me with his thick cock, filling me with long, slow strokes. "Madi..." His voice is rough. He sounds lost.

He unties my wrists and hoists my torso up, so I can rest on my hands, giving him access to my breasts. He plays with them, pinching and rolling my nipples as he bumps my ass with his loins.

I close my eyes, my cells alive and vibrating. This man has always been able to play my body like a maestro. He produces a symphony of sensations that become too much to track individually. The sex I had before Brick was like the jangled notes that come from an untuned violin in a beginner's hands. I had no idea the explosive possibilities pleasure could hold before him.

I'm reveling in it all when he pulls out. "On your back, Windows. I need to see your face when I make you come." I roll onto my back, and he enters me again. "That's it." He rocks into me and caresses my cheek. "So beautiful."

His eyes glint yellow. As he stares down at me, I fear he sees everything. How much he means to me. How afraid I am of believing this is real. Of trusting him enough to let go and let him in.

I must be right because he pins my wrists beside my head and says, "You're still holding back. How do I conquer you–the sassy assistant who brought me to my knees?"

I try to hold onto my heart, which has grown wings and is attempting to fly out of my chest.

"I don't want to be conquered." My voice sounds raspy. Broken.

"No, you don't, do you? You know my secrets, but you won't give me yours. What does it take to win your heart?"

I blink back the moisture in my eyes. Turn my head to the side to escape the torture of his scrutiny. Brick steadily rocks into me.

"Take me." He punctuates the words with thrusts, but I suspect this is more than dirty talk. "Take all of me. Receive me. Let me in. I want you, Madi. I want you to want me as much as I need you."

I moan beneath him. Writhe against the hold he has on my wrists. The hold on my heart. His words pierce me, wound me, *brand* me. They bring me to orgasm—a rolling slow one that starts with a squeeze and ends with me screeching and yanking Brick's hips into mine with my legs behind his back.

He bucks against me, thrusting forcefully, making the bed bounce and rock and slam against the brick wall. His eyes glow pure wolf, and I swear he nearly howls when he comes.

"Brick."

"Madi."

We speak each other's names like we're each describing our particular brand of heaven.

"Brick."

"Madi."

Like we're finding each other in the dark.

Like we've been lost and alone and just found the one person in the world who knows who we really are.

"You're a wolf," I murmur in awe, remembering. Honoring.

"You're everything," he whispers back.

* * *

Brick

"Don't get up," I murmur when the doorman downstairs calls up about the food arriving. I slip on a pair of pants and pull on a t-shirt. "I'll be right back."

"Are we eating in bed?" she calls after me.

"Yes."

I don't ever want her to leave my bed. I'm going to keep her naked and available to me for the rest of the night. And tomorrow morning. In fact, we can ditch work and stay in between the sheets all day long.

That thought puts a cocky smile on my face as I open the door and accept the large bag of food. When was the last time I smiled? I can't even remember.

All I know is my wolf is tremendously soothed by having Madi in my place. I love having her scent on my skin, her taste on my tongue. I know bringing her home doesn't solve my bigger problems, but it's a temporary reprieve from the need that was tearing me apart.

It buys me time while I figure out how to make this work. I wanted to mark Madi when we had sex. Or rather, my wolf did. It's time to accept the fact that my wolf chose a human as his mate. I need to claim her forever as mine. I have to trust that nature knows best, despite the destruction mating her could bring on my life.

I need to talk to my team. I need them onboard with this. By my side. Maybe there's a way to keep Madi and the pack. There has to be.

I grab a couple forks from the kitchen and carry the food back to bed, along with bottles of the fancy water I like. Madi rolls her eyes when she sees them. She's sitting up in my bed, the sheet wrapped around her waist, her skin flushed like she's a goddess.

"Oh my God. You have the same water here? You really do like it."

"Of course I do." I unscrew the cap and hand one to her.

"I thought maybe that was just one of those ridiculous challenges you set up to test me. Like the 6 degrees Celsius thing."

My adorable, brilliant assistant. "You didn't fall for any of it, did you?"

Her smile is unguarded. Warm. "You must know by now that I love a challenge."

"I do." I open all the containers and spread them

175

between us on the bed. There are seven in all–steak, salmon, two different salads, scallops, chicken, and pasta. "Take your pick, Windows."

She reaches for the salmon. I note her choice with interest. I want to learn all her quirks. What she likes. What she hates. What I can do to make her life fulfilling.

My wolf is desperate to take care of her. To feed her, protect her, satisfy her.

He's desperate to mark her, but it's far too soon for that. She just found out I'm a wolf. I'm not about to explain the entire fated mate situation and the fact that my wolf needs to sink his teeth into her and embed my scent in her delicate human flesh to prove she's mine. Marking a human is a dangerous business–another reason shifters and humans don't usually mix. She doesn't have the natural healing properties wolves do. My bite will cause her lasting pain and permanent scars. If I hit an artery, it could kill her. Then, there's always the chance of infection.

I pick up the container with the steak and devour it. Shifting makes me hungry as hell.

"Is your helicopter pilot a wolf?" Madi licks a drop of sauce from the corner of her mouth and my dick goes hard again.

"Acker? No."

"So that's why he was placed in the servant's quarters at Thanksgiving, too?"

I take the empty container of food from her hands and set it aside on my bedside table. "They weren't servant's quarters. I told you that before, Windows. I wanted you as far away from me as possible because of your scent."

"What about it?"

"It drives me insane."

She blinks at me. "In a good way?"

176

"In an insane way. Like an itch I can't scratch."

"I'm an itch you can't scratch?"

"You've been the worst kind of temptation to me, Madison Evans. Sassy and smart with this citrus and spice scent that makes me want to devour you." I fist her hair in the back to pull her face to mine for a kiss.

The scent of her arousal blooms between us.

"What about Genevieve?"

"What?" I'm thinking about kissing those lips until they're swollen, but of course Madi's still putting everything together in that genius brain of hers.

"Is she a wolf?"

"No. Just a well-paid HR exec."

I watch her as her mind turns. "Jerry!" She lifts her gaze to mine in triumph.

"The janitor? Yes. How'd you guess?"

"He doesn't follow the same rules as the other janitors. He doesn't wear the uniform. Indira said there are certain people who seem like they get special treatment at Moon Co."

"That's because I trust wolves more. Jerry is the only janitor I allow on the executive levels to clean. There's too much at risk to trust a human."

"I'd like to unpack that prejudice with you at some point, but I have too many immediate questions."

I stack the uneaten food containers on the floor beside the bed. "Ask away, Windows."

"Does it hurt?"

"What? Shifting? No. I mean, it's not always comfortable, but it doesn't hurt."

"Will you show me your wolf again?"

I smile indulgently and stand up from the bed to remove my clothes. Madi sucks in a sharp breath when I shift, drawing back. I jump up on the bed beside her. She tentatively reaches for me and strokes my fur.

"My what big teeth you have," she murmurs, but when I smile, showing more fang, she yanks her hand back like she's afraid.

I shift back, chuckling.

"Does the government know?"

"There are some incidences of government captivity and testing on our kind. An attempt to create super soldiers or something. There are also private collectors and crazy scientists who have captured shifters for their personal gain. There's a clandestine group called Venators who capture shifter juveniles to hunt them when they first shift."

"That's...horrible."

"Yes. Two more questions, and then I'm going to ravish you again."

Her eyes light up. "Are you?"

"Yes. Scratch that. You're out of questions. I need to be inside you again."

It's not hyperbole. My wolf wants to mark Madi with a desperation I feel all the way in my bones. Sex is the only answer. I just need to tide him off with lots and lots of sex.

Chapter Sixteen

Madi

Madi

Driving into Moon Co with Brick is a surreal experience. He pulled a Big Bad Boss on me and insisted I "work" from home with him yesterday, which basically meant staying naked in his bed and getting pleasured so often my throat went hoarse from crying out.

This morning, he drove me to my apartment and picked up lattes for us while I changed into fresh clothes.

Basically the last thirty-six hours have blown all my synapses. Werewolves exist. And vampires. And my boss is not just the Big Bad Boss, he's the Big Bad Wolf.

He pulls into the office building's garage and parks.

I feel like I should duck down and hide, so people don't see me driving in with the boss. I mean, how much more obvious could it get?

"I shouldn't walk in with you," I say as we walk toward the elevator.

"You're mine," Blackthroat growls, almost like he's responding to some invisible threat. "No one is going to interfere with us."

I don't know why it makes my lips tremble and my eyes burn.

The moment we step off the elevator, though, the bliss-bubble I'd been in bursts.

The top floor is filled with Brick's execs loudly talking over one another. All eyes turn to us and silence descends. My paranoia kicks in. Is this about me? About Brick dating a human?

"What?" Brick snaps.

"You couldn't check your phone at all over the last twelve hours?" Nickel asks.

No, it's something else.

"Try thirty-six. What is it?"

"There's been a security breach. We had to shut everything down to contain it."

"Fuck." Brick transforms into a formidable boss, storming into the room. "How did it happen? What do we know?"

"Come into the conference room," Billy says. There's something stony and cold about the way he speaks that makes the hairs stand up on my arms. "We have something to show you."

"Madi." Brick delivers the one-word command for me to follow.

"*Not* Madi." Billy holds up a hand and blocks our path.

"*She comes,*" Brick snarls, and Billy almost stumbles backward, like the force of Brick's words or will pushed him.

I remember the way my body seemed to move of its own accord with Aiden Adalwulf and wonder if it has something to do with their alpha status. I make a note to ask Brick later when we're alone.

The execs close in on us as we walk in, every one of them assembling at the table with grim faces.

I'm usually calm here at work, no matter what the stress. I had that detachment thing down pat. I didn't care about the job or getting fired, and it made it easy to function in a demanding situation.

All that has changed now, though. I find myself trembling, scared for Brick about whatever it is his team is about to show him. Because I can tell it's bad. Bordering on horrible.

"What the fuck is going on?" Brick can tell, too.

There's a file folder in front of Billy, and he lays a hand on it but doesn't open it. He looks at me. "Madi, since you're in here, maybe you can tell us what's going on."

My heart thuds, even though I have no idea what he's talking about. All I can tell is that this is an ambush, and I need to catch up, fast. "I don't know what you mean." I try to make the words sound even, but even I can hear I'm rattled.

"How long have you been working as an Adalwulf plant?"

The shock of the words registers far less than their effect on Brick. The color drains from his face, and he pushes away from me to take in my face.

I try to swallow but my mouth is dry. "I haven't."

"No? Aiden Adalwulf called this morning to ask if Brick enjoyed the gift from his mate."

Brick stiffens even more. No, I think he turned to stone.

"What are you talking about?" I croak.

"We know the breach was initiated from your computer, Madi. My PI team followed you, and I have video of you meeting with Aiden Adalwulf in front of the building. I have phone records proving you've been having conversations with him. I also know you let Catherine Adalwulf onto the top floor and left her unsupervised to roam around."

"Okay, that doesn't prove—"

A wounded animal sound comes from Brick as he stands and backs up, like he's afraid he'll throttle me if he stays within reaching distance.

"What was your motivation in infiltrating Moon Co? Did they pay you? Or was it part of your Occupy Wall Street efforts?" He slips out the photo of me and Aubrey sitting on the sidewalk holding Occupy Wall Street posters that he must've taken from La Résistance.

"I'm not a plant. I've barely even spoken with Aiden Adalwulf—"

"Don't say his name," Brick roars. His eyes flash with a bright light.

Billy flips open the folder and spills a number of photographs onto the table. There's me standing, facing Aiden Adalwulf that day he caught me on the street.

It does look bad.

"This is nothing. He cornered me, tried to offer me a job. I said no."

Brick's whole body is taut. He runs a hand through his hair, making it stand on end, wild.

I turn to speak directly to him. "I said no, Brick. You have to believe me—"

"We also traced phone calls coming from Adalwulf Associates' to your personal line," Billy interrupts. "Several calls, in fact."

The weird phone calls I got when Brick was in California. "Those weren't—"

"You've also entered Adalwulf Associates' building before. Do you do deny it?"

"No, I went in to get coffee. I did nothing wrong."

"There's no need to act all innocent," Billy sneers. "We've got you. We know you're responsible for the breach."

"I'm not. I don't know anything about it. Brick, you know me." I focus on him. Brick, the Big Bad Boss. The man–werewolf–I'm coming to love.

Last night we were together in bed, and he was so sweet. Rough in the best way, but also tender.

Surely with everything that's gone between us, he knows me. He knows I'm loyal. I would never betray him.

After a long pause, Brick shakes his head. He looks past me to Billy. "Lock everything down. Get her computer to Jake and his top team, look into the breach."

I sag like I've been punched in the chest. I wish it had been a punch, it wouldn't be as painful as this. *He doesn't believe me.*

"Already on it." Billy's smile is triumphant.

"Brick." I take step forward towards him.

"Don't come any closer," he rasps, gripping the chair so hard his knuckles go white. There's a crack as the plastic breaks. I freeze, trying to comprehend what's happening. He just broke the chair with his enormous strength.

"This isn't just Moon Co," he says.

"What do you mean?"

"I can't be with you. I have to choose my pack. *I have to.*"

"Hang on," I say. "I don't know anything about the security breach. I swear. Occupy Wall Street was a long time ago, and the only reason I was talking to Aiden Adalwulf was because–"

"*I don't want to hear it!*" Brick roars. His eyes glow completely yellow. "Somebody get her out of here now."

My heart thunders with distress. Tears fill my eyes. I had always pictured my last moments at Moon Co, doubting I'd last, and I'd sworn I wouldn't cry the way that first assistant had. I'd sworn I would never care. Yet here I was not just caring, *dying*.

"Brick." I hate the pleading tone in my voice, but I can't mask it. I can't hide what he's come to mean to me. I'm not just losing my job, I'm losing everything.

"I'll escort her out." Billy stands from the table, his posture so menacing I flinch.

"Not you," Brick snaps. He flicks his finger like he wants to left-swipe me right out the door. "Nickel."

Nickel walks silently over to my side and extends his arm toward the door in a charitable gesture of showing me the door.

I stand on shaky legs. Stand and stare at Brick whose blazing eyes show only his wolf.

"Brick?" I try one more time. This time there are tears in my voice. I don't even care how much I'm humiliating myself. I want him to know I didn't do this. I would never hurt him or Moon Co.

"Let's go, Madi," Nickel says in his crisp English accent. He takes my elbow and leads me out the door. The first tears fall the moment we cross the threshold.

"Pack your desk," Nickel clips.

"I don't want anything," I mumble, only stopping to pick up my coat before heading straight for the elevator.

The tears continue to slide down my face in the elevator ride down to the first floor. I somehow manage to hold the sobs in and keep silent, but I can't breathe.

"Give me your employee badge." Nickel holds out his hand.

I fumble in my purse and pull it out to hand to him.

"I didn't do it," I croak when we reach the bottom.

"I don't care," Nickel answers.

The elevator doors open, and he walks me all the way to the front door where he tells the doorman that I'm not allowed back in.

I stumble out on the sidewalk. Sleet hurls from the sky like further punishment.

Like God is saying, *This is what happens when you let your guard down, Madi. When you trust a rich man.*

This is what you get.

* * *

Brick

Rage storms through me with flashes of red and white. I'm surprised I didn't already shift, but then, my wolf wouldn't attack Madi. Not when he believes she's his mate. I wanted to throw the conference room table through the windows when I found out, but my wolf wouldn't let me do that either. He wouldn't even let me hand her over to Billy, knowing how much he hates her.

Now I know how my father felt, to be mated to the enemy. It's a wonder he survived as long as he did. The impossibility of my parents' situation has struck me many times over the years but never more fully than now.

Every single time my father looked at my mother's face, he had to know she wished to betray him. She was the enemy, yet he still couldn't stop himself from seeing her. From claiming her. From taking her up to his bedroom every week when she visited.

Ultimately she destroyed him. And he accepted his death from her hand. He probably knew it would come one day. He probably expected it from the first night he claimed her.

Once Madi is gone, I overturn the giant mahogany table. I smash every chair against the wall, crumpling each one to the size of a cabbage.

Then I turn and face my team. "Get the breach under control," I say. "We need to be back up and running today."

"That may not be possible," Vance says.

"Make it possible!" I rage. *"And I want every detail about how this happened written up, so we can go over it."*

My friends eye me warily.

"Somebody get me a fucking helicopter right now." I need to shift and run within the hour or somebody will end up bloodied on this floor.

"I'll call Acker," Jake offers.

"I'll tell Genevieve about the change in personnel," Vance says.

"I don't want another assistant!" I shout. "No one—no human—ever steps on the top floor again."

Chapter Seventeen

Brick

I may not survive this.

It's that thought above all else that eventually forces me to turn back to my human form and get my ass back to Manhattan.

Vance insisted on coming with me to the Berkshires, despite the fact that I threatened to tear out his throat if he wouldn't leave me alone. I ran my wolf for thirteen hours straight there until I collapsed and Vance dragged me back into the cottage.

Liz and Dane were frantic, trying to feed me, get me in the shower, and make sure I didn't go back out to run. Nobody spoke a word about Madison Evans, and for that I have to be grateful.

They all fear I'll go moon mad.

I fear it, too.

This situation was like a human getting a stage four cancer diagnosis. I'd met my mate, my wolf had chosen, and now he was being denied. A wolf with as much alpha power as I carry can't survive such a blow. I don't know if I'll even make it to the full moon. Not with this much rage and betrayal swimming around in my head.

Knowing my pack and company need my leadership right now, especially if I'm going to go feral by the full moon, I am in the office by morning in a suit and tie, ready to take heads.

Getting off the elevator to a silent top floor is too much, though. I stop and stare at Madi's empty desk with bitterness. The office still smells faintly of her orange and Frankincense scent. I swear I almost detect the scent of her tears from the day she left, but that's just my brain producing a memory.

The memory makes my chest tight.

I don't mean to, but I walk over to her desk and stand above it. Not to catch her scent. Just to make sure she's cleaned all her belongings out.

She hasn't. Her tube of hand lotion still sits beside the phone. A lip gloss is next to the computer. There's a greeting card standing behind her monitor that reads, *You're killing it*. I snatch it up and open it.

It's from her brother. Inside he wrote, "I didn't get you a graduation present, but I saw this and thought of you. Congratulations on the Moon Co job. You're killing it!"

My chest hurts even worse. The memory of Madi drunkenly poking my chest that night her band played, telling me she knew I'd paid for her brother's tuition surfaces.

I want to villainize her. Demonize her. But just like my mother, she's someone I loved first, before she ripped my heart out.

It's not black or white. Good versus evil.

She's a real person with emotions and insecurities and

people she cares about–like her younger brother. Her friend Aubrey.

I'd stupidly thought she cared about me, but it turns out it was all a lie.

Still, it's hard to untangle the love from the hate.

I pick up her desk and hurl it at the wall, then stalk into my office and call Vance. "I want all the execs working on the top floor until this gets resolved," I bark.

I can't stand being alone up here. It will hurtle me to madness even faster than I'm already going.

My team streams in and updates me.

The programmers have figured out how to patch the system and Moon Co is up and running again, but our stock price dropped a hundred million overnight. Nickel is working his ass off doing interviews and sending new press releases to try to get it to bounce back.

I sit and listen and then fold my hands. "Okay. What do we know about the mechanics of the breach?"

"We still only know that it came from Madi's computer. It looks like she loaded it the night of the holiday party, and then it was set to activate at a later date or was remotely activated."

I blink, hit with a torpedo in the center of my chest.

The night of the holiday party.

The one where I drove her home and spent the night at her apartment. And she broke things off with me.

"Find out which it was. I need to know everything about how this happened."

"What about the Adalwulfs?" Jake asks.

"What are you asking?"

"They need to pay for this." His gaze burns with vengeance.

"Yes." This goes far beyond me scooping up the land

they wished to purchase. They tried to take down my entire company, same as they took down my father's. "They certainly do. But we have more pressing concerns right now. We need contingency plans in place for leadership of the pack and the company."

"What for?" Nickel asked.

"You know what for."

Billy goes pale. "Are you saying..."

I nodded gravely. "Madi is my mate. My wolf will drive me to madness for refusing her. I'm already losing control."

"I told you," Vance mutters to Billy.

"What about Thaddeus?" Eagle suggests, standing from his chair and pacing around the conference room.

Thaddeus is Manhattan's vampire king.

I hesitate. Wiping Madi's mind of the existence of wolves is probably necessary, but the idea turns my stomach. She's so young and bright. It could ruin that genius mind of hers.

"I don't just mean wiping her mind. I mean..." –he looks grim– "control it. You need her to surv–"

My hands close into fists, and a growl rockets from my throat.

Billy watches me like I'm a lunatic with a loaded gun. "Table that for later," he says in a low voice to Eagle without taking his gaze off me.

"*No.*" I put an alpha command into my voice, and everyone in the room falls back a few inches. I know exactly what Billy's thinking. They're going to talk about Madi in private and bring her to Thaddeus without my consent since my wolf will never allow it.

"Nobody touches her. You will not go around me on this. Understood?"

It isn't just my wolf making the demand, not that it's

always clear where my thoughts originate. No, I'm sure I would rather die than have Madi trotting around here as a mind-controlled zombie just so I don't go mad.

No one answers at first. They all like the idea. I probably would, too, if it came down to losing one of them to human treachery.

"*I said no!*" I thunder.

My team remains silent.

"Perhaps you should consider marking her and *then* discarding her. That would alleviate the greatest risk of madness," Nickel suggests.

"No." This time it's crystal clear who's talking. Me–the proud, stubborn man who would rather hold a grudge and die than make any kind of peace with the woman who betrayed me. My wolf is totally on board with marking her. Now. Yesterday, in fact.

"I don't wish to discuss Madi. I will draw blood on the next person who brings her up. I want to talk about the pack and the company."

"We're looking at complete and utter devastation," Billy says. "There will be no Blackthroat pack. None of us are strong enough to hold it. No one will trust me over you. The only reason they trusted you at age eighteen is because your father made it clear that you were his successor and all the wolves who fell in behind him backed you. Only one or two families defected. This time they will all defect. The Adalwulfs will pick off the weaker factions."

Concerned looks ping-pong around the table.

"Contingency plans for the company, then. Let's get to work."

* * *

Madi

I stay in bed for two days without eating or sleeping. On the afternoon of the third day after being fired, I finally start following the loops and turns my mind has been hashing through while I've been wallowing in bitterness and despair.

The thing my brain kept returning to was that meeting with Aiden. When I realize why, I sit up abruptly from bed. Shower. I need a shower.

I swing my legs over the side, stand up, and nearly pass out because I haven't eaten in two days. I'm sure I look like a holy terror. I'm in an old worn T-shirt and panties, and my hair is a tangled mess from lying in the bed with the covers over my head.

"Hey, you're up." Aubrey comes into my room. Her voice is soaked with sympathy, which makes me want to dive back under the covers for another cry.

But no. I figured something out.

"I need food," I manage to say.

"I've been telling you that." Aubrey snatches up the store-bought smoothie she brought in for me earlier this morning from the bedside table and gives it a shake. "Here, drink this."

I uncap it and suck down half the contents. "Thanks. Listen–" I pace into the living room of the apartment. "We have to do something."

"Yeah. Let's plot revenge on those entitled assholes."

"No!" I wave an impatient hand. "Listen–I was framed."

Aubrey looks at me like I've lost my mind. "Obviously."

"No, I mean, I think I know how they did it."

"How?"

"The janitor." I punctuate the word with a jab to the sky with my index finger.

"Let's get you some more food," Aubrey says, like I've lost my mind.

Okay, maybe it does sound too hokey. Too Agatha Christie tidy. But I just remembered the thing that was bothering me.

"He was the only one who could've known when I was leaving the building the night Aiden tried to get me into his limo. He's also one of the few people who has access to my computer. And he's a wolf."

"A what?"

Oops.

Too late I realize that I've said too much.

Even after Brick throwing me out, I still would never reveal his secret.

"I mean, he was probably working for the Adalwulfs."

"Oh. Yeah, he could be. Is that all you have on him, though? That evidence is pretty circumstantial."

I tap my lips. "There's the private investigator Brick hired to find out if Eleanor Harrington was my grand-mother. I could call him. Maybe he can find a record of a payment from the Adalwulfs to the janitor. Or something?"

Aubrey looks at me doubtfully. "Well," –she shrugs– "I guess it's worth a shot. But why are you doing this? Do you want your job back?"

I hate that my eyes fill with tears. I thought I was done crying over this. "No, I don't want my job back. But I also can't stand Brick thinking I would do this to him."

I'm not obtuse enough to miss the parallel he was led to draw between his mother's betrayal and what he believes is mine. He jumped to conclusions because of his past. That wound is so deep, and this whole fiasco just fed into it.

That's the sick part. Aiden Adalwulf went for his deepest wound when he used me to get at Brick. I mean, he didn't use me–I wasn't a willing participant in his treachery–but he framed me for this whole thing. Used my computer. Staged a meeting with me in front of the building. Made the phone calls damning me.

What had Aubrey said to me back when I was in the Berkshires? *Never date a man who hates his mother?* She couldn't have been more right. A man who hates his mother believes every woman is out to get him. Every female is going to be damned in his eyes.

Which makes me think...

Suddenly it all sharpens into focus.

Catherine Adalwulf's insistence that she was innocent. Her desperate attempts to explain herself to Brick and repair the relationship. Could it be...?

Aiden knew how to play this game because it's been played by his pack before.

Catherine Adalwulf has been a pawn in her pack's feud against the Blackthroats. A pawn like me.

An even greater sense of resolve to get to the bottom of this mess comes over me. Enough wallowing. It's time to get back in there and repair what's broken. I have no intention of ever speaking to Brick again, but I can't let the Adalwulfs win this round. No.

If I can clear up this farce they've laid out for Brick to believe, I will.

"I'm going to take a shower," I say. I need to come back to the land of the living. I'm sure I stink, and I know I'm not very pretty to look at right now.

"Cool." Aubrey heads into the kitchen. "I'll make us lattes for when you get out."

* * *

Brick

Moon Co has been on lockdown for almost a week dealing with the security breach.

The executive team is stationed on the top floor as we manage the crisis. Or possibly they're just trying to manage me. My sanity is as much of a crisis as the fate of the pack and company right now.

Sully calls me after hours. I'm still in the office. I'll probably sleep here again. "What is it?"

"I had an interesting phone call."

"Don't speak in riddles," I snap. "Why are you calling?"

"Madison Evans."

Dammit.

My wolf roars to life. He wants to kill Sully for even mentioning her name. As if Sully might be moving in on our mate. Courting her. Stealing her from us, which of course is absurd, since I've already cast her aside. "What about her?" I snarl.

"She contacted me. She has a theory about a security breach. She believes it was enacted by the janitor, Jerry. She noted he had the opportunity and means to infect her computer as well as to notify Adalwulf of her comings and goings, so he could time a meeting in front of her building."

I go still. My fangs are already descending to rip Jerry to shreds.

"Have you looked into her theory?"

"I'm sitting in front of his place right now. I didn't find any record of monetary rewards, but he has made phone calls to Aiden Adalwulf's phone. I checked with Billy to get the time of her reported meeting with Adalwulf and guess what?"

I can't form words. Only growls come from my throat.

Fortunately, Sully goes on without my reply. "One of the calls came twenty-five minutes before the timestamp on that video of the meeting."

I hang up the phone to howl, ripping out of my clothes and spontaneously shifting.

Billy barges in my office.

I barely manage to shift back without attacking him. I know Billy is trying to protect me, but he may have jumped to a false conclusion about Madi.

And I stupidly believed him.

I need all the facts. I glower at him as I stuff my legs in a new pair of boxer briefs and suit pants. "Send me the video feed of Madi with Aiden and get Noah up here."

He studies me, wary. "It's nine at night–Noah probably isn't in the building."

"I don't fucking care! Find him and get him in my office within the hour." I blast Billy with enough alpha command to make his body sway.

"Yes, Alpha."

He leaves the office, and I find an undershirt to pull on. Then I put my fist through the wall. I falsely accused Madi. Well, Billy did, and I believed him.

Just when I almost had it figured out–how to somehow keep her and still maintain the safety of my pack. Now I may lose both.

Forty minutes later, I hear the elevator ding, and I throw open my door to see Noah enter with Billy.

Nickel and Eagle emerge from the conference room.

Noah takes in the mess I've made of the office. Madi's desk is lying on its side after I flung against the far wall, the contents scattered all around.

He appears alarmed, looking around and sniffing. For Madi?

My wolf wants to kill him.

"She's not here."

Noah inclines his head. "How can I help?"

"In my office," I growl.

Noah enters, and apparently Nickel, Billy, and Eagle think that's invitation enough for them to come in as well.

They take in my torn-to-shreds office. Ribbons of fabric are scattered about the room from the times I shifted while fully clothed. The walls have claw marks and several of the chairs are broken.

I stand behind my desk and point at my computer screen. I'm sure I look deranged.

I *am* deranged.

"Noah."

The younger man watches my lips move.

I beckon him over to my side of the desk. "You read lips."

He nods.

"Can you look at this video and tell me what they're saying?"

Noah winces. "Videos are hard. Lip reading is only thirty percent accurate. Under normal circumstances my shifter senses and context clues improve that, but with a video, I may not get much."

"I understand. You can only see one of their faces, but the lighting is decent because he's under a streetlight. Will you try?"

"Of course."

He presses play on the video, and we see Aiden Adalwulf in a long woolen coat on the sidewalk near Madi's building. He watches it several times. "I think he said, *How much does he pay you?*"

Madi walks into the frame.

My wolf goes insane at the sight of her, and I nearly shift again.

Noah darts an alarmed look my way. Whether it's because I seem dangerous and close to feral right now or whether he's just putting two and two together about Madi being gone and the video of her speaking the rival alpha, I can't guess.

Her back is to the camera, so Noah can't see her lips to read them.

Noah watches it several more times. "He's saying double–maybe that he'll double it."

He lets it play and rewinds to rewatch. "I think he's asking if she's fucking her boss." He darts another look at me.

My upper lip lifts, and I let out a loud snarl. "He's insulting her."

Noah nods. "It seems so. Then he says something about a secret–*did he tell you his secret?*" He rewinds and reviews a few more times. "And then something like, *he doesn't plan on keeping you.* I don't know–the last part is tricky. He says that she's smart or not smart. Not smart enough."

The tendons in my neck harden, and I'm sure my eyes turn amber, but I manage to nod.

Good, I remind myself. This is good news. It's proof it wasn't Madi.

How could I have ever believed Madi would be working for Aiden? She's loyal to the core. She may be defended, but she truly cares about me.

And I lumped her in the same category as my mother.

I couldn't have fucked up more.

"Thank you, Noah."

"Was it a help?"

I give a grim nod. "Yes. I've made a terrible mistake." I shove my hands in my pockets. Some of my insanity has leaked away. I feel calmer than I have in days.

"But that's actually the good news."

Chapter Eighteen

M*adi*

Brick started calling last night. I didn't answer. It's Christmas Eve, and I managed to drag myself out today to get a few presents for Aubrey, my mom, and Brayden, and now I'm holed up at the apartment.

Tomorrow, I will go to my mom's to be with my family, but I am just not ready to fake holiday cheer yet tonight.

I heard on NPR that Moon Co's deal with Benson was approved. Indira tried to call me a few times over the last couple of days, but I wasn't up to chatting.

I did my part to get closure. I talked to Sully about Jerry, and I called Catherine to tell her what had happened and commiserate on our similar fates of being used by her pack to harm the men we loved.

Now I am done. It's time to move on although I don't know what that means.

I have the money from the bonus Brick gave me, and I've saved a large portion of my salary, so I don't need to rush off and find a job. I can take my time to lick my wounds and figure out what I want to do.

My phone buzzes with another text from Brick. The first read, *"Madi, please pick up your phone*; then, *I made a terrible mistake*. Followed by *please let me apologize."*

It's tempting to answer. To hear the apology. My pride wants to soak it all up. But my heart just can't take it. The pain of this breakup was like nothing I've experienced in my life.

It's honestly something I never, ever want to go through again. If that means I put my heart on the shelf and never sleep with another man or woman, so be it. I seriously can't take pain like this again. It would kill me.

Aubrey walks in and throws her pea coat over the arm of the coat rack by the door. "Save me." I thrust my phone out. "I don't want to answer his calls or texts."

She stomps over in her combat boots. "I got you." She takes my phone and walks away from me, her thumb moving across the screen.

Of course, my control issues rear up. Or is it fear of letting go? "What are you doing?" I call after her.

"I'm blocking him–that's all. He doesn't even deserve a response."

"Wait." I jump up from the couch.

She darts into the bathroom, closes the door, and locks it.

"Aubrey!" I shout, trying the handle even though I heard the door lock. "Wait."

"Too late. All messages and voicemails have been deleted, and the number is blocked." The door unlocks, and she breezes out, an impish smile on her face. She hands me the phone back. "Problem solved. He won't be bothering you again."

I try to ignore the sense of panic that brings on. But it

was the right thing to do. I am not ever going back to Moon Co or speaking to Brick Blackthroat again.

End of story.

Aubrey puts on her Christmas movie, *Die Hard*, which isn't helping my mood. I don't need a sexy, growly hero or villain right right now. Still, it's better than being alone, so I stay to watch with her.

Forty-five minutes later, our door buzzer sounds.

I look at Aubrey with a sense of panic rising in my chest. I'm usually so in control, but today I'm having a hard time managing my emotions.

"It's okay," she says. "I ordered Chinese food for us."

I lean back against the couch and exhale, but when Aubrey opens the intercom line, it's Brick's voice that barges into our living room.

"Madi?"

I shudder at the gruff bark of his voice. Not because it doesn't sound wonderful to my ears.

Because it does.

I was a fool when I was with him not to realize just how deeply I'd fallen in love. It was only obvious after I lost him.

"Madi's not available," Aubrey answers in a falsely pleasant voice. She glances at me as she goes on, "And this is a No Billionaires Allowed building, so please vacate the premises."

She releases the intercom button, so he can't answer, but he starts ringing the bell incessantly.

"Can we disconnect the thing?" I jump up and stalk toward the intercom.

Aubrey bodychecks me out of the way. "Don't even think about coming near this." She hits the intercom again. "Don't make me call the police. Madi's not here, and even if she were, you're the last person on Earth she would talk to. Goodbye!"

"Disconnect it," I hiss when she releases the button.

"But our Chinese food!"

Right. Damn.

Miraculously, he doesn't buzz again.

Instead, his name pops up in my personal email box. I guess he got the address from my resume. I delete it without opening it.

He's sorry. That's honestly enough. I feel vindicated. I don't need to read his words or hear his voice for more because that would only make me go running back to an impossible situation.

Twenty minutes later, the Chinese food arrives. Aubrey buzzes the guy up, and he knocks on the door.

I jump up to get it.

Big mistake.

Of course, it's Brick, looking half-mad. His hair stands on end, his rumpled button-down looks like he slept in it.

He stands there holding our Chinese food. He must've paid the delivery guy off to get in and bring it to us.

All my senses are hit at once. His dangerous beauty. His clean scent. The way I long for those large hands to touch me.

I'm like a deer in the headlights, unable to speak or move. Just struck dumb. "No," I manage to whimper.

He attempts to step forward, but I block the door. His eyes glint amber. "Hey. May I come in?"

Aubrey barrels up off the couch. "Nope, nope, nope. I'm calling the cops. Get out of here now." She snatches our food from his hands, plants her hands on his arms and attempts to move him.

I remain frozen until Aubrey's brow wrinkles in confusion at her inability to even budge the guy.

"I know, he's really strong," I say quickly to stop her from trying. I shift my gaze to him and find his pinned on my face. "But he usually understands the meaning of the word no."

"Madi, I'm sorry I didn't believe you. I fucked up. Will you please give me a chance to grovel?"

"Out!" Aubrey shouts.

I force myself to remain dead, no matter how tempting it is to leap into his arms and let him grovel his way over every inch of my body. "You heard her."

"Madi, there's more afoot here than you know. I need to explain some things to–"

"No," I interrupt. "You really don't. I never belonged on Wall Street, and we both know I didn't belong with you. So, please, just let this go. I accept your apology. I'm glad you know it wasn't me. That's closure enough. Thanks and bye." I swing the door shut on him.

He still doesn't move. He looks deranged. "Five minutes. Just give me five minutes and–"

Aubrey joins me, and we both push on the door, trying to force him out.

"I don't have a lot of time."

Seriously? What an asshole. "Then you best be going."

Aubrey holds her phone to her ear. "I'd like to report an attempted assault."

Brick withdraws, and the door slams shut with both Aubrey's and my weight against it.

"Are you okay?" she asks softly as I struggle to breathe.

"Did you actually call 911?"

"No, do you want me to?"

I shake my head and rally. I can get through this. I'm

strong. I'm smart. The pain will eventually go away, I know that. I manage a nod.

We pick up the boxes of food from where Aubrey had set them on the floor and crawl onto the couch to watch the rest of the movie. I can't choke down more than a few bites of rice, but eventually this gnawing anxiety will leave my belly.

I hope.

It's not until the middle of the night that I remember what Brick had said about vampires and wiping my mind.

* * *

Brick

I stand in the boardroom, my hands planted on the glass, and stare at my own reflection. My eyes are bright as lasers and I'm glowering hard enough to carve through this window and the Adalwulf building beyond.

If I look down, I can see Moon Co and everything I've worked for, laid out at my feet.

I'd raze it all to the ground if it meant I could get Madi back.

She rejected me. I don't blame her—and I can't have her even if she was willing to be with me. An alpha can't mate a human.

There are voices outside the conference room. Nickel, Jake, and Vance, murmuring.

"Is he—"

"Yes. Still no change. He ordered us to leave him."

"Should we bring him home?" Vance asks. "It's Christmas."

I snarl. I'm not leaving the office. I've gathered every

personal item and scrap of furniture that still bears her scent, and my wolf won't allow me to leave it.

Nickel quickly shoots him down. "We can't risk someone seeing him in this state. No one can know."

If the Adalwulfs found out I'm this out of control, they'd go for the jugular. It'd be all out war, and they'd use the news of my weakness to rally their feral pack and kill as many of my pack as possible. They've wiped out packs before–killed the leaders, absorbed the rest into their ranks. My pack is strong, but without me as a figurehead? The largest families would leave, and the pack would splinter into weaker factions the Adalwulfs will see as easier prey.

I have to hang on to my sanity. Too many lives hang in the balance.

I have to fight this.

I clench my fists. My nails have sharpened to claws and cut my palms. The blood drips, staining the carpet. Staining my suit.

And what does it matter? Without my mate, there's nothing for me.

My wolf rises and fur ripples along my forearms. I'm so tired of fighting him. I have so much to fight for–my pack and family–but my wolf doesn't care. He knows what I'm beginning to believe.

Without Madi, I have nothing.

* * *

Billy

"We have a problem." Vance calls me the day after Christmas.

With most of my pack mates in the Berkshires for

Christmas, I spent the day yesterday with my parents at our family retreat in Vermont. Now I'm on my way to work after the first good night's rest I've had since the security breach.

It's hard to imagine we could have *another* problem. The security breach has been the biggest shit show since our previous alpha got murdered by his own mate back when we were at Yale.

"What is it?"

"Madison won't talk to Brick."

"Why is this our problem?" I snap. Solving lovers' quarrels really isn't my area of expertise. Especially not when a human's involved.

"He didn't go to the Berkshires for Christmas. He's been here at Moon Co all night and..." Vance sighs. "He's acting erratic. Like he keeps putting her hand lotion all over his face. He's truly losing it."

I tunnel my fingers through my hair. Losing Brick is not an option. "Fuck. So he tried calling? Going over there?"

"Yeah. He sent her a giant trophy that said he was sorry, which didn't make sense to me but whatever. She refused it. She also turned away a van full of roses."

I roll my eyes. For fuck's sake. Humans and their methods of courtship are utterly ridiculous. Why couldn't Brick have picked a wolf? Literally any she-wolf in the world would've been better than this. Hell, even a he-wolf would be better–who cares if they can't reproduce?

"What does Madison want? Actually, it doesn't matter what she wants. We just need Brick to mark her."

I hate the idea of him marking and mating a human, but things have gone too far. This may be the only way to save his life now.

"Agreed." Vance seems to have arrived at a similar

conclusion. "We need to get them in the same room to figure this out."

"Yeah. Okay. I think we should revisit the plan that involves the vampire king." Thaddeus could mind control Madi into coming to see Brick and submitting to a claiming bite. Once that is complete, the two could work the rest out on their own.

Vance goes quiet, considering.

It's a good plan. One that would solve everything, especially now that we know Madi isn't working for the enemy.

Eagle and Sully have our real traitor, Jerry, imprisoned in Sully's basement right now. We may or may not have worked him over thoroughly with our fists when we put him there, not that pain matters much to a shifter.

"He wouldn't be able to come until after dark," Vance says.

"Obviously."

"That's nearly eleven hours from now."

Alarm bells clang in my head. I scrub a hand down my freshly shaven jaw. *"You don't think he'll make it eleven hours?"*

"It's not looking good."

"I'll get the human," I say.

"How?"

"I don't know–I'll knock her out and carry her if I have to."

"Bad idea," Vance cautions. "You even touching her could flip the switch in him. We have to think this through carefully."

"I'll talk to her roommate." I *am* thinking carefully. That ridiculous roommate is key to solving this dilemma.

"Okay, good luck with that. I'll loop the rest of the guys in on the Thaddeus plan and see if we can get a consensus."

"Yep." I end the call and change lanes. My car drives straight to La Résistance like it knows the way. Like I've driven here already a hundred times in my mind.

Which of course, I haven't. Because why would I?

I find a place to park and walk two blocks to get to the cafe. As I pass by, I give the mural on the outside wall a scornful look. This hippie shit is over the top and ridiculous. Then I see the signature.

Aubrey Jane Cook.

Huh. I take another look at the artwork. I hate the subject, but I have to admit she's talented. Proportions are perfect, the colors pop. Not that I care about things like that.

I push through the door of the cafe and spot the room-mate behind the counter. Even with all the scents of food and coffee, I detect her unique scent in the air, and it does something unnerving to my blood.

She sees me, and her brown eyes flash. Her jaw thrusts forward in anger.

Okay. She remembers me.

She extends an upturned palm when I get to the counter although I have no idea what she's demanding. Shrugging, I fish a twenty dollar bill from my pocket and drop it in her hand.

She yanks her hand back like the money scalded her. "My picture." She jerks a thumb at the bulletin board. "You stole it."

"Ah. Yes, indeed. I borrowed it. I will bring it back."

She folds her arms across her chest. Her long braids shift over her slender shoulders. "What are you doing here? Just out ruining lives for fun again?"

My lips twitch. Not because I find her words amusing but because I love her anger. I must truly despise humans because my cock actually gets chubby seeing how much she hates me.

"I came to solicit your help."

"You must be out of your mind. You'd be the second to last person on Earth I'd ever help. The very last would be your buddy, Brick."

"Well, that's unfortunate because he's the reason I'm here. Something very important has come up at the office, and he needs Madison."

She cocks her head. "He should have thought of that before he chose to believe your lies about her and had her thrown out of the building. You don't come back from that."

"It's extremely important and only she can help. I'll give you fifty thousand dollars if you convince her to go. Deposited in your bank account today."

It was the wrong thing to say. This is the girl who occupied Wall Street. Money's not a good motivator. Her upper lip curls in disgust. "Absolutely not. Get lost." She makes a shooing motion with her hand. Her fingernails are an unmanicured disgrace, with blue paint caught around the sides and underneath them.

I want to catch that hand and fold it behind her back. Bend her over the counter and spank her ass. I bet it would satisfy on many levels. Especially if it made her mad. I want to lean closer and sniff her neck. Find the place where her scent gathers and lick it.

"Five hundred thousand." I can't stop myself, even though I know it won't move her. Know I'm botching this. I want to see that flash of anger in those dark eyes.

Her nostrils flare. She shakes her head. "You really are a piece of work."

"I'll make the same deal with Madi–tell her that. She likes money."

Aubrey draws back like I slapped her. "She *does not*."

I shrug. "Let her decide for herself."

Aubrey narrows her eyes at me. "Are you done?"

"Yes." I pick up the discarded twenty dollar bill and drop it in the tip jar. "Thanks for your time."

As I walk away, my shifter hearing picks up her angry mutter. "Entitled alpha-hole."

Even though I failed my alpha, I still can't help feeling a spurt of satisfaction from her words.

Brick

I'm losing my ability to think rationally. I've managed to stay in human form today, but I'm not even sure why anymore. My team flits around, sending me worried glances as I pace around the first floor.

"Brick," someone says. "*Brick.*"

I turn. It's Vance. Billy stands beside him. "Come into the conference room," Vance beckons.

I follow because I'm not able to do much leading right now.

"Madi's coming tonight," Vance says.

The fog in my brain suddenly clears, and my mind sharpens. "She is?"

"Yes. We'll bring her here as soon as we can. And then you can mate her."

I frown, suddenly realizing that everything is wrong about this conversation. The way they're looking at me. The idea that someone else would bring Madi to me.

My fangs start to descend. "Nobody touches her," I snarl.

"I told you not to tell him yet," Billy mutters.

"What?" I whirl. My eyes must be glowing because my vision is sharp as hell.

Billy holds his hands up. "Hey, it's going to be okay. We'll get Madi for you. Thaddeus will–"

I cut him off with a roar. Billy's the asshole who made me believe Madi had betrayed me in the first place. Now he's not heeding my orders to keep Thaddeus away from her.

I shift and leap through the air, my fangs snapping for his throat.

* * *

Madi

The day after Christmas, my phone rings. It's Ruby. I decline the call. She immediately rings back. After four rounds of it, I finally pick up. I have no reason to dodge her calls, after all. Talking to her won't cause more physical pain in my chest. It's already there every breathing second.

"Hi Ruby."

"Madi!" She sounds frantic. Like emergency-level frantic.

I suck in a sharp breath.

"Madi, listen. This is a life or death situation. Where are you?"

My heart revs up to Olympic speeds. "Is it Brick? Is he okay?"

"No!" She sounds hysterical–like she's holding in a sob. "He's going to die, Madi, and only you can save him. I'm on my way to your apartment right now. Are you there?"

I may or may not have stayed in bed all day again. I throw the covers off and climb out. "Yes, I'm here."

"Can I pick you up in twenty minutes? Please, Madi.

After tonight, you never have to see him again, but we really need you right now. Brick needs you."

Oh, God. What could it be? How can I save Brick from death? I run for the shower. "Yeah, I'll be ready. I'll wait outside." I end the call and turn on the water for the shower, stepping in before it's even warm.

My hands tremble. What could it be? Car accident? No. Why would they need me for that? Besides, he told me they had superhuman healing abilities.

Something with the Adalwulfs, then?

It still doesn't make sense. I rush through a quick shower, then dress and dash downstairs.

A limo pulls up to the curb, and I climb in the back with a tearful Ruby.

"What's going on?"

"Oh, Madi, thank you so much for coming." She throws her arms around me.

I have to fight my own tears back because I know once I start, they won't stop. "What happened? What is it?"

"Brick has gone feral. It can happen to alpha males who don't claim their mates by middle age."

I blink, trembling. Not understanding but waiting for more.

"His wolf chose you as his mate. He waited too long to claim you, and now he's succumbed to moon madness." Tears stream down her face. "It may be too late, already, but I'm hoping you can bring him back."

Dammit, now my own tears leak from the corners of my wide eyes. "Bring him back from what?"

"From his wolf state. He's gone feral," she repeats, and it starts to come together for me. Goosebumps raise on my arms.

214

"So he can't change back? Or won't? Is that what feral means?"

"Yes. Exactly."

I draw in a measured breath, trying to get control of my panic. Trying to find the Madi who's great in an emergency. The one who thinks on her feet.

But she's freaking out, right with Ruby. Brick can't die. He *can't*.

"Where are we going? To the Berkshires?"

Ruby shakes her head. "No, he shifted at Moon Co again. They locked him in the conference room, but he's tearing the walls down to get out. If he does…" Her eyes are wide and horrified.

"If he does, *what?*" Alarm clangs through me.

"He'll have to be put down."

My empty stomach heaves. I feel like bursting into full-on sobs, too, but I keep it together. Brick needs me. I'm his mate. I'm not sure what that means, but if I can save Brick, I will.

"It's okay," I promise, even though I have no idea if that's true. "We'll save him."

When we get to MoonCo, I forget to feel awkward or stiff about getting fired and returning now. All I can think about is Brick being put down. We get off the elevator on the top floor, and I'm shocked by what I see.

My desk has been thrown to the far side of the room. Trash litters the floor. The ferocious snarls of a wolf, terrible scratching sounds and the thud and clang of heavy objects being thrown emanate from the conference room.

The executive team lingers in the main area, and they appear relieved to see me.

"Good work, baby." Eagle pulls Ruby into his arms.

"This way, Madi," Nickel clips in his crisp English. "Thank you for coming."

"Of course I came," I say hotly, but then I realize with a sick feeling that Brick was trying to talk to me about this. He needed my help, and I turned him away. Refused his calls. Shut him out.

Oh, God.

Hot tears threaten again. I'm responsible for this situation.

Nickel leads me to the conference room where Sully stands outside the door, loading a gun.

My eyes fly wide. "What are you doing with that?"

"These are silver bullets," Sully says grimly. He screws a silencer on the muzzle. "They will take him down if necessary. It's a last resort, obviously."

My fear level ratchets up to atomic levels. The door shudders with the impact of a very large animal hitting it, followed by an unearthly howl.

"He hears you," Nickel says.

"Brick?" I call out.

"Don't," Sully cuts in. "Don't rile him up. He'll think we're keeping you from him." He cracks the door. "She's coming in," he calls through the door. "Back the fuck up, bro." He opens the door and peers through before stepping in and making room for me to follow. He folds his arm across his chest, the gun resting on his heart.

"What are you doing with that?"

"I'm going to protect you." His jaw clenches, but when he looks at the giant wolf growling at us, his eyes take on a sheen. He means kill Brick.

"The hell you are," I snap and point at the door. "Get out of here."

At the sound of my raised voice and anger with Sully, the wolf goes mad, snarling and barking, lunging at him.

"Easy, easy, easy." He holds his hands out. Thankfully, he doesn't point the gun at him. Yet.

"Get out!" I yell.

Sully backs toward the door but presses the gun into my hands. "Take this."

"I'm not using that." I try to push it back.

"Take it. Don't put it down. Keep it pointed at him. If he lunges at you, shoot him straight between the eyes."

"Get out!" I scream.

The wolf leaps at Sully, but he slams the door just in time, and the great beast hits the wood, his claws scraping down it.

I'm shaking all over. How much of the Brick I know is still in there? Has he gone totally mad?

"Brick?"

He makes a grumbling sound, trotting around the room in agitation. He's like one of those caged animals at the zoo that make you wish zoos and cages never existed.

The room is destroyed–claw marks everywhere, cracked windows. The chairs look like they've been through a trash compactor. It's utter devastation. There's blood on the floor and table. I'm not sure who it belonged to.

I am completely out of my depth here. How do I calm a wolf? How do I appeal to the man inside? This isn't some graphic novel where I sing him a lullaby, and he calms down enough to change back.

Tears fill my eyes. My back hits the door, and I slide down. "Brick, please."

The wolf stops pacing and stares at me. There's nothing about the giant animal that reminds me of Brick. Nothing to make me feel safe here.

The hairs on the back of my neck stand up at his continued stare. Does he recognize me? Is he going to attack?

"You're scaring me." I hold the gun with shaking hands, sloppily pointing at him.

He lowers his head, trots over and whines.

I let out a shaky exhale. "Yeah, it's me. Do you recognize me?"

He sinks to his belly and inches forward, into my personal space. When he gets close enough for me to touch him, he rolls to his back and whines.

"Brick." Tears of relief streak down my cheeks. I set the gun down and gingerly reach out to rub his belly.

He licks my hand.

"You need to change back now. Can you hear me, Brick? Your friends and your sister are terrified. You really went on a rampage this time."

He shivers and leaps to his feet again, his fur ruffling across his neck and shoulders like he's angry.

"What did I say?" I eye the pistol on the floor, but don't pick it up. "Come on, you have to shift back."

He comes back to me, but is more aggressive this time. He bites my pants and pulls, ripping a hole in my leggings, then lunges toward my throat but only licks my ear. It's not an attack. At least...I don't think it is. It's more... an aggressive show of affection.

Then suddenly, he's a man, pushing me onto my back, his hand at my throat.

"Brick!" I'm alarmed again. His eyes are still golden, his canines seem longer than human teeth. The weight of his body pins me to the floor.

"Please, please, please, Madi." He sounds hoarse. "I need you." He rips my leggings and panties off.

Oh. Um. Okaaaay.

"Please... my control is... " He pushes my knees up and licks into me. His fingers join his tongue, and he rubs roughly. "I need inside of you. Please, Madi."

"Brick." I'm still more than half-scared of him. He's panting. His eyes are wild. He's definitely not himself. Probably still dangerous.

"Life or death," he manages to choke out as he rises above me, his fingers already penetrating me, stroking. "You're wet for me. Please, Madi. I don't know if I can hold off the change much longer."

Life or death. Having sex with me will save this man's life. Truly, I have a magic pussy. Now I suddenly understand why Brick was so passionate before. How he needed to have sex the moment he walked into the building.

I grip his shoulders. Reach for his dick to guide him in.

He lets out a roar when he sinks into me and starts moving with a frenzy.

It's terrifying but also delicious. To be so desired, so wanted by a man is a heady experience. "Mark... I have to mark...*Madi.*" He shakes his head like he's trying to get control. "I'm going to bite you."

"Wait... what?" I don't know what he's talking about.

"Please don't freak out. I promise I will make it up to you. I'll be careful. Won't go too deep." He's already lowering his head to my shoulder, those gleaming canines definitely longer than man-teeth. "It's the only thing...save my life."

He has to bite me to save his life.

How can I refuse? "Okay. I understand." My voice quavers with fear. "Do it."

He shudders and his teeth sink into the place where neck meets shoulder. I gasp. It burns and throbs like a mofo, and for a second I go into shock. But then I realize Brick is in the throes of pleasure. He shakes and shudders, orgasming.

The pain instantly morphs into pleasure. I buck against him, my own unexpected orgasm crashing over me. I wrap my legs behind his back and hold him in against me, my inner muscles squeezing and contracting around his cock. A hoarse cry flies from my lips.

The door behind us flies open, and I hear several people invade the room with cries of alarm.

Brick extricates his teeth from my trapezius muscle.

"Get out."

* * *

Brick

My friends back out of the room and shut the door to give us some much-needed privacy.

I lick Madi's wound to prevent infection and try to keep all of her body shielded from view as I glare up at my friends.

"Thank fuck," Nickel says from the other side of the door.

I get it. I was inches away from a painful, silver-bullet induced death. I almost couldn't find my way back. My human form is exhausted from fighting my wolf. It's the relief that comes after a long hard battle. An all-out war.

It was only Madi's beautiful voice that cleared my head enough to shift.

"It's okay, he's back." Eagle says outside the door–probably to Ruby.

I roll to the side and pull Madi into my arms. "I'm sorry.

I'm so sorry. I couldn't stop myself. You saved my life, baby. Thank you so much."

Her lips tremble, eyes brim with tears. Her face is pale. "Ouch."

"I know. I'm sorry, sweetheart. It's a mating mark. I know I fucked up. I fucked everything up. Thank you for coming."

She pushes against my chest. "I came for Ruby." She's still mad at me. It doesn't surprise me that someone with such a strong will and firm convictions would also be unwavering in her decision to cut me off forever.

But she came. She let me mark her. Her eyes shine with tears, so I know she still cares. Know that this stems from the pain I inflicted, not logic.

"We're done." She scrambles away and collects her torn panties and leggings, wobbling as she tries to step into them.

"Madison—Madi. I don't trust easily. It's a terrible flaw, I know that."

She manages to get both legs through the holes and yanks up the combined set, frustrated when the panties wrap around and get trapped halfway up.

"I should have trusted you. I *do* trust you. You got set up by Aiden, and I believed the worst, but I won't make that mistake again. Please don't walk out that door."

She stops with her back to me, her hand on the doorknob. The wound from my mark stands out, angry and red, the edges still open, seeping a little blood. My need to tend to her, to take care of her, nearly bowls me over.

"*Please*. I won't make the same mistake again. Not ever. I just marked you as my mate. Wolves mate for life, Madi. You're the only woman for me. Please don't walk out that door."

She turns and looks over her shoulder, and the uncertainty in her expression guts me. I'm the one who made her so insecure about our relationship. I wouldn't give her anything but orgasms. I refused to admit she was my mate. Refused to own up to what she meant to me until it was too late. So when the Adalwulfs used her as a weapon against me, we had no foundation to stand on. The shifting sand beneath our feet made it possible for me to believe she'd deceived me.

I climb to my feet to persuade her and spread my hands. "Please." I gesture around the trashed conference room. "You mean everything to me. All this is a result of not mating you."

I know the moment I've won because she takes the time to look around the room.

She cocks a hip. "I don't know who you expect to clean this up, but if you hired a new assistant–"

I catch her up around the waist and pull her against me. "I didn't." I lick her wound again to provide immunity and speed healing, then brush my nose against hers and seek her gaze.

She melts against me.

"I'm sorry, Madi. I was an ass. Please forgive me."

She melts a little more and nods. "Yeah, I'm a little sorry I refused the giant apology trophy you sent."

I chuckle, relief wending through my veins. "I'll have it re-delivered tomorrow morning."

"You didn't hire a new assistant?"

"How could I?" I ask softly. "No one will ever compare to you."

She sweeps her gaze down my naked body, taking in my dick, which is already standing at attention for her. "I'll get your suit."

I catch her arm and tug her back against me. "You don't have to serve me."

"Don't take away my fun."

I chuckle. Right. She has a boss kink. I can't forget that. "Well, snap-snap then." My tone is a suggestive rumble.

She's ever-efficient, opening the door a crack to peek out and order my friends like the queen she is. "Can someone get us a set of clothes from the closet there?"

I hear the relief in the voices outside, and all I can do is drink in the sight of Madison, my beautiful mate, back in here where she belongs.

Chapter Nineteen

M^{adi} I'm Brick Blackthroat's fated mate.

Also, I'm in love.

It feels insane to admit what has been true for a long time.

I guess I've always protected my heart, except around the few I completely trust. Aubrey. My mom. Brayden. That's it.

But now, it feels like my entire chest has been blown wide open. My heart is swinging in the wind with no protection.

No guarantee.

But knowing Brick's wolf needs me to survive is a pretty strong assurance he'll stick around. He's not going to abandon me like my rich, asshole sperm-donor did.

"Tell me more about this mating bite." I gingerly touch the swollen puncture marks in my shoulder. I'm on my back in his bed, and Brick is sucking my toes, one by one, determined to deliver me to death by multiple orgasms.

We've been holed up naked in his apartment for two days now, and every minute, I fall more and more in love.

"It means I claimed you, Madi. I embedded my scent permanently into your skin. Every shifter who comes near you will know you belong to me." The moon shines through the glass of the window, bathing the bed in pale light, making Brick's eyes glow amber.

"*Belong* to you? What century is this?"

"It means I belong to you, then." The warmth of his gaze on my face makes my heart flip-flop in my chest. "A mated wolf will do anything for his female. *Everything*. Your happiness, safety, and sexual satisfaction are now my highest concern."

There's so much for my brain to wrap around. I'm still trying to assimilate it all.

"So it's like the shifter form of marriage?"

"Yes. But it's far more intense than a human pairing. Wolves mate for life. They only have one fated mate. That mate is everything to them."

"Like Eagle and Ruby."

He kisses up the inside of my ankle, sending tingles straight up my inner thigh to my core. "Actually, they aren't fated mates. Their love was conventional. The human variety. Eagle fell in love with the pack princess at a young age and worked his ass off to prove he was worthy of claiming her."

"Oh." I digest this information.

"My father wouldn't condone the mating, but after his death, I allowed it."

"You *allowed* it?"

Brick grins. "Ruby is pack royalty. If I forbade the mating, Eagle would've had to challenge me, and he would've lost."

"Medieval."

"Yes. But I was a young alpha. Eagle made himself indispensable to me and was a rock for Ruby. There's no way I would've denied their happiness. Especially not after watching my parents' miserable mating."

"So...Ruby doesn't have a fated mate?"

Brick shrugs. "She might have one out there somewhere. I think both of them fear one of their true fated mates will show up and blow their lives up."

I stare at Brick. "That would be terrible."

"Yes. But finding one's fated mate isn't guaranteed. And as you know, when a male wolf doesn't mate by the time he reaches his prime, he runs the risk of going moon mad. Eagle and Ruby were meant for each other whether their biology clicks as fated mates or not."

My mind reels as I take it all in. I remember what he told me about his parents–the Romeo and Juliet of rival packs. "So your dad needed your mom to stay alive, but they were sworn enemies."

"Yes, exactly. Ruby, Scarlet and I were born from a loveless match."

"It's so crazy. You would think the three of you–their offspring–would be the ones capable of joining the two packs together."

"Yes. That's exactly the prophecy the Adalwulf's seeress had and why they had to orchestrate my father's murder before I was old enough to lead."

"But you did lead."

Brick's jaw hardens. "Yes."

I stroke away the tension in his face, pull him down for a kiss. Our tongues mate and tangle. Brick pushes me to my back and climbs over me, nudging my thighs open once more.

"I guess stamina isn't a problem for wolves." I grip his cock with my hand and guide him in.

"Stamina will never be a problem when you're in my bed, Madi." He pushes in deep, then eases back and repeats the action. "I have a perpetual hard-on if you're in the same room."

"Don't forget I'm human." I rock my hips up to meet him.

He instantly freezes. "I'm sorry, sweetheart. Are you sore?"

I grip his hips and pull him back in. "Yes, but it feels good."

He moves slowly, without aggression, keeping his gaze locked on mine. My belly flutters with the intensity of it. My body heats. My heart glows.

This is what it means to be desired. To be truly cherished. To be loved.

Brick's eyes begin to glow amber. He picks up speed, but still keeps it gentle. Still trains his gaze on mine, holding me captive to receive the intensity of the moment.

Of his promise. He's mine now. I'm his.

This is what it feels like to be important to Brick Blackthroat, my billionaire boss. The werewolf of Wall Street. Alpha of his pack.

The man I thought endangered my heart is actually the one person I'm safest with. Because I'm his one and only.

His fated mate.

* * *

Brick

I wake surrounded by Madi's sweet scent. The watery winter light slants over the bed, illuminating her angelic

228

face. For the first time in months, my wolf is content. All because of her. The human assistant who turned my life upside down.

Madi. My mate.

Mine.

I'm debating how I should wake her, when her eyes slit open, and she yawns. "Morning."

"Good morning." I gather her close, noting how she winces when she moves. Humans aren't meant to have mating bites, but whenever I check the puncture marks to make sure they're healing, I get so aroused I can't resist putting her on her hands and knees and claiming her all over again.

I have to be careful with her, though. She survived my savagery and faced down my feral wolf and took everything I gave her in bed for the past few days, but she's probably still sore. She deserves some care and tenderness.

"How are you feeling?"

"Good." She stretches in my arms. "What time is it?"

"Time to get up." I roll her to her side and lightly smack her ass. "You'll be late to work, and you've said yourself, your boss can be a real dick."

Her giggle is like champagne bubbles in my bloodstream. "If I'm late, do you think he'll punish me?"

A wave of desire takes my breath away. "Always." I lean down and claim her lips, drinking her in. She's all I ever wanted. All I ever needed. And I'll never get enough.

I'm seconds away from ripping away the blanket, rolling her to her back, and filling her up when she pulls away and swats my shoulder.

"Enough. I need something to eat. And a shower."

I show my teeth, ready to dominate her, but her

stomach growls. The sound saps my strength. She's the center of my world now, and her needs are my priority.

Sex can wait. I need to take care of my mate.

"Shower first." I rise and help her up, wrapping her in the blanket, so she's not cold. "I'll order some food."

I grab my phone, and it lights up with an incoming call. Eagle. I have a bunch of missed calls from him and the others, including Billy who's still on my shit list. They'll be wanting to know I'm all right.

"Go on in," I urge her. "I'll join you."

"Please do," she murmurs, and the smile she shoots me over her shoulder makes me want to chase her down and take her right on the floor.

Down, boy. No sense having a mate who's too sore to walk. Although it would be a good excuse to keep her in my bed...

My phone buzzes with a voicemail and lights up again. Eagle's going to keep calling until he hears my voice. I grab my phone and answer. "What."

"Alpha. Thank fates."

"What's happening?" The water for the shower goes on, distracting me, and I lope across the room to the windows overlooking Central Park, so I can focus on this call.

"The Adalwulfs are what's happening."

That gets my attention. What now? We have the breech contained. "What did they do?" My voice drops an octave, my wolf snarling through. We have a mate to protect.

"It's bad." Eagle sounds exhausted. "They released footage of your wolf in the boardroom."

"What? When?"

"Last night. One of Aidan's cronies must've taken it when you two sparred. An email went out to everyone in our pack. It doesn't show you shifting from human form to wolf. But everyone in our pack knows what your wolf looks like. They know it's you. They know you were out of control."

My mind is already spinning, evaluating.

This is bad. Really bad. Things are shifting toward Aiden's favor. I will not allow the Adalwulfs to win again.

Not on my life.

"All right. Let's issue a statement, do some damage control–"

"It's too late for that. The pack's in chaos."

Fuck.

I close my eyes. The worst thing I could imagine is happening.

Eagle continues, "The top families in the pack have already called for a town hall meeting. Your top wolves all stand by you, you know that. Nickel and Ruby have also met with the most volatile agitators, told them you're still our alpha. You still lead the pack."

"Of course I do. Why wouldn't I?"

Eagle hesitates. "They think you're moon mad over some human." He doesn't add, *Because you were.*

"No. I'm not." Not any more. That problem has been solved. I head to my closet to get dressed. "When is the meeting? I'll be there." A show of strength, that's what I need. I'm almost recovered from the moon madness. I could fight if I had to.

"Is that wise? Some of the younger ones want to challenge you. No one wants to defect, but they have to know you'll lead us."

A growl erupts from my throat. "I am alpha. I lead the pack. I will destroy any challengers."

"All right." Eagle sounds relieved. He probably was

worried my top wolves would have to fight all challengers for me.

"Meet me at the office," I tell him. "You and Nickel. We'll send out a broadcast. Round up some of the heads of families, see if we can meet with them before the meeting or one by one to prove I'm still their alpha. We'll want all the support we can get before the pack-wide meeting." I can fix it. I held the pack together by the skin of my teeth when my father died. I can do it again.

"And what about the human? You going to tell everyone about her?"

My brain races as I consider my options. I can't reveal anything about Madi to the pack. Not if they already think I'm weak. She'll have to remain my secret.

"As far as anyone's concerned, she doesn't exist. I fired my human secretary, like all the others. It's no big deal." Eagle hears the lie in my voice but doesn't say anything. He'll help me sell it to our pack. "I'm still in fighting form. We've uncovered the spy and the Adalwulfs plot and removed the threat. We're stronger than ever."

"So we cover up everything that happened? The fact that the human's your..." he hesitates. He doesn't want to say it. "Your mate?"

"What mate?" There's a pang of guilt in my gut at rejecting Madi like this, but it's for the greater good.

I was born an alpha, born to lead. I can't allow anyone to distract me from that.

Not even her.

"Tell Sully to send two of the enforcers downstairs up to guard the door to my penthouse. I need Madi safe."

"Done." Eagle ends the call.

"Brick?" She appears, wrapped in a towel. "Weren't you

going to join me?" She sees me buttoning up my work shirt, and her playful grin drops away. "What's wrong?"

"Nothing. Pack stuff."

"Pack stuff? What–"

"It's handled." I cut her off. My wolf hates that I'm being rude, but I don't have time to explain the intricacies of pack hierarchy right now. Not when my pack is about to implode. "I'm heading into the office."

"Okay. How can I help?"

"You can't." I grab a suit jacket and shrug it on. I don't bother with a tie. If things go south at the pack meeting, I might have to fight a few upstarts for dominance.

"Okay. I'll get ready... Do you have anything I can wear to work?" She's trying to sound teasing, maybe make a joke about keeping a stash of peek-a-boob dresses here in my closet but can't quite manage it.

"You're not going."

Her head jerks back. "What?"

"I'm sorry, Madi, but you're not going back to the office–not today, not ever."

Her face goes white like I've slapped her. "You said you didn't replace me." Her voice is dangerously quiet.

"It's not safe for you out there. We're under active attack by the Adalwulfs. And no, there's nothing you can do to help. You're not a part of it. You can't be–you're human. "

Her expression hardens, her walls slamming into place. I see the moment when all the trust, all the beautiful intimacy between us goes up in flames. She presses her lips together, her eyes narrowing.

The anger in her scent riles my wolf even more than the threat to my pack, but there's nothing I can do to fix it. I'm the one who's made her angry.

"I see." She heads for the bed, grabbing her yoga pants and putting them on under her towel.

I can't bear to watch her close down, shut me out. I force myself to turn and head for the door. "I have to go."

My wolf whines like he's been wounded. But he knows we have no choice. Madi is safe and secure here. We have to protect our pack.

She's fully dressed, and on my heels. I whirl and pull her close, pressing a kiss to her forehead.

I'm sorry, I want to say. But I can't. Because I have to choose my pack.

One day, she might understand.

* * *

Madi

I push Brick away, incensed. "So, I'm still fired?"

His expression is pained. "For now. You can't come to work. The situation's...delicate."

Delicate? I am perfectly capable of problem-solving all the sticky situations that arise for him. Even when I was falsely accused, *I* was the one who solved the mystery.

"And I can't be trusted with the details? Have I not proven I can solve any problem?"

Brick's expression is unyielding.

My face gets hot. "I can't believe this." I push past him and grab my coat.

"Where are you going?"

"I'm not staying here."

"You can't leave."

Warning bells clang in my head. "What do you mean? I can't go home?"

"No. I have to keep you safe. And a secret."

"What?"

"Madi... our mating...it has to be a secret. No one can know."

My stomach caves like he punched me. My throat goes dry.

"You're human. My mating you won't be acceptable to my pack. I could lose everything."

I can't believe this. It's just like my mom and Brett-fucking-Harrington. I'm not good enough to be presented to society. But in this case, it's wolf society.

I'm going to be sick.

"You're a weakness to the pack. My weakness."

I'm ice cold. "Screw this." I yank open the front door.

Brick moves fast, somehow getting through the door first to block me.

Two beefy men stand outside like sentries. "Good morning, Alpha," one of them says gruffly.

"Tell no one that she's here. Guard her with your life. No one gets in" –he turns to give me an unfathomable look– "or out."

"What?" He can't mean that. I harden my voice. "You can't lock me in here, Brick Blackthroat. If you leave me here now, I'll never forgive–"

The door shuts. Only my pride keeps me from rushing forward and beating on it, cursing the man who made me such beautiful promises. Promises that didn't last a week.

I'll be calm. Logical. I step forward, ready to try the door. I can reason with Brick and solve this dilemma just like I've solved every other one.

But my strength gives out when I hear the cold, final *click* of a deadbolt, and I realize I'm locked in. I'm a bird in a gilded cage. A princess in a tower.

Trapped.

Betrayed.
Utterly alone.

* * *

Thank you for reading *Moon Mad*! Read the conclusion of Madi and Brick's saga in ***Big Bad Boss: Marked***. One-click *Marked* now —> https://geni.us/bbbmarked

Marked

RULE #3 OF WALL STREET: NEVER SHOW WEAKNESS

Grab it now! https://geni.us/bbbmarked

Want FREE books?

Free Renee Rose books:
Go to http://subscribepage.com/alphastemp to sign up for Renee Rose's newsletter and receive free books. In addition to the free stories, you will also get special pricing, exclusive previews and news of new releases.

Download a free Lee Savino book from www. leesavino.com

Other Titles by Renee Rose

Paranormal

Wolf Ridge High Series

Alpha Bully

Alpha Knight

Step Alpha

Alpha King

Bad Boy Alphas Series

Alpha's Temptation

Alpha's Danger

Alpha's Prize

Alpha's Challenge

Alpha's Obsession

Alpha's Desire

Alpha's War

Alpha's Mission

Alpha's Bane

Alpha's Secret

Alpha's Prey

Alpha's Sun

Shifter Ops

Alpha's Moon

Alpha's Vow

Alpha's Revenge

Alpha's Fire

Alpha's Rescue

Alpha's Command

Werewolves of Wall Street

Big Bad Boss: Midnight

Big Bad Boss: Moon Mad

Big Bad Boss: Marked

Alpha Doms Series

The Alpha's Hunger

The Alpha's Promise

The Alpha's Punishment

The Alpha's Protection (Dirty Daddies)

Two Marks Series

Untamed

Tempted

Desired

Enticed

Wolf Ranch Series

Rough

Wild

Feral

Savage

Rebel

Warrior

Vegas Underground Mafia Romance

King of Diamonds

Mafia Daddy

Jack of Spades

Ace of Hearts

Joker's Wild

His Queen of Clubs

Dead Man's Hand

Wild Card

Daddy Rules Series

Fire Daddy

Hollywood Daddy

Stepbrother Daddy

Master Me Series

Her Royal Master

Her Russian Master

Her Marine Master

Yes, Doctor

Double Doms Series

Theirs to Punish

Theirs to Protect

Night of the Zandians

Bought by the Zandians

Mastered by the Zandians

Zandian Lights

Kept by the Zandian

Claimed by the Zandian

Stolen by the Zandian

Rescued by the Zandian

Other Sci-Fi

The Hand of Vengeance

Her Alien Masters

Also by Lee Savino

Paranormal romance

The Berserker Saga and Berserker Brides (menage werewolves)

These fierce warriors will stop at nothing to claim their mates.

Draekons (Dragons in Exile) with Lili Zander (menage alien dragons)

Crashed spaceship. Prison planet. Two big, hulking, bronzed aliens who turn into dragons. The best part? The dragons insist I'm their mate.

Bad Boy Alphas with Renee Rose (bad boy werewolves)

Never ever date a werewolf.

Tsenturion Masters with Golden Angel

Who knew my e-reader was a portal to another galaxy? Now I'm stuck with a fierce alien commander who wants to claim me as his own.

Contemporary Romance

Royal Bad Boy

I'm not falling in love with my arrogant, annoying, sex god boss. Nope. No way.

Royally Fake Fiancé

The Duke of New Arcadia has an image problem only a fiancé can fix. And I'm the lucky lady he's chosen to play Cinderella.

Beauty & The Lumberjacks

After this logging season, I'm giving up sex. For...reasons.

Her Marine Daddy

My hot Marine hero wants me to call him daddy...

Her Dueling Daddies

Two daddies are better than one.

Innocence: dark mafia romance with Stasia Black

I'm the king of the criminal underworld. I always get what I want. And she is my obsession.

Beauty's Beast: a dark romance with Stasia Black

Years ago, Daphne's father stole from me. Now it's time for her to pay her family's debt...with her body.

About Renee Rose

USA TODAY BESTSELLING AUTHOR RENEE ROSE loves a dominant, dirty-talking alpha hero! She's sold over two million copies of steamy romance with varying levels of kink. Her books have been featured in USA Today's *Happily Ever After* and *Popsugar*. Named Eroticon USA's Next Top Erotic Author in 2013, she has also won *Spunky and Sassy's* Favorite Sci-Fi and Anthology author, *The Romance Reviews* Best Historical Romance, and has hit the *USA Today* list fifteen times with her Bad Boy Alphas, Chicago Bratva, and Wolf Ranch series.

Renee loves to connect with readers!
www.reneeroseromance.com
reneeroseauthor@gmail.com

 facebook.com/reneeroseromance
instagram.com/reneeroseromance
bookbub.com/authors/renee-rose

About Lee Savino

Lee Savino is a USA today bestselling author, mom and chocoholic.

Warning: Do not read her Berserker series, or you will be addicted to the huge, dominant warriors who will stop at nothing to claim their mates.

I repeat: Do. Not. Read. The Berserker Saga.

Download a free book from www.leesavino.com (don't read that either. Too much hot, sexy lovin').

Made in the USA
Coppell, TX
15 August 2024

36054183R00152